Heirloom Kitchen

HERITAGE RECIPES AND FAMILY STORIES
FROM THE TABLES OF IMMIGRANT WOMEN

◆

Anna Francese Gass

PHOTOGRAPHS BY ANDREW SCRIVANI

HARPER
DESIGN

An Imprint of HarperCollins Publishers

Heirloom Kitchen
Copyright © 2019 by Anna Francese Gass
Photographs copyright © 2019 by Andrew Scrivani

HarperCollins books may be purchased for educational, business,
or sales promotional use. For information please email the Special
Markets Department at SPsales@harpercollins.com.

Published in 2019 by
Harper Design
An Imprint of HarperCollinsPublishers
195 Broadway
New York, NY 10007
Tel: (212) 207-7000
Fax: (855) 746-6023
harperdesign@harpercollins.com
www.hc.com

Distributed throughout the world by
HarperCollins Publishers
195 Broadway
New York, NY 10007

ISBN: 978-0-06-284422-4
Library of Congress Control Number: 20199322423

Interior design and hand-lettering by Laura Palese Design
Recipe testing by Monita Buchwald
Food styling by Alexandra Utter

Page 57: photograph courtesy of Bob Kidd Photography
Pages 96 and 106: photographs courtesy of Rod Gleason Photography
Personal ephemera and photographs used with permission from each respective family

Printed in the United States
First Printing, 2019

To my family

Phil, Alessandra, Veronica, Dante, Mom,
Dad, Luciana, Chris, Gigi, and Maxie

◆

*Everything I accomplish is due
to you holding me up, working it out,
and cheering me on.*

Contents

INTRODUCTION

Once upon a meatball

♦

This story begins, as many great ones do, with a meatball.

I GREW UP in an Italian-American household in Rhode Island, which meant I lived my outward life as an "American," but at home, I was surrounded by the sounds and smells of Italy. When I came home from school, there was usually something simmering on the stove as my mother asked me about my day, and our weekly meal rotation included all the dishes my mother grew up eating in Italy. Because she was brought up on home-cooked meals, she didn't understand the concept of premade food or the frozen food aisle of the grocery store.

However, after endless requests for "American" food from my sister and me, she obliged. One day, she begrudgingly threw a frozen chicken pot pie in the oven, and we waited impatiently and excitedly for it to brown. Finally, it landed on my plate with a thud. We tentatively picked at it with our forks, only

to realize it was crisp on the outside and frozen solid on the inside—inedible!

To this day, we chuckle about that childhood memory, because my mother can cook a six-course meal from scratch without batting an eyelash, but ask her to make a processed, frozen dinner and she will fail every time. She had no interest in exploring the fast, prepackaged foods readily available to her after moving to the United States. Instead, she viewed her new American identity as an extension of her Italian identity, and she was intent on preserving the food traditions of her homeland, no matter how laborious they were in comparison to the meal practices of her new home.

Cooking "her" food is a large part of my mother's identity. She is known for making delicious, home-cooked dishes that were taught to her in a tiny countryside kitchen in Calabria by her mother, Grazia, and grandmother, Angela, who were each taught those recipes by their own mothers and grandmothers in turn. Each recipe has a story, a lesson, and, of course, a delicious taste. Although I grew up a world away, visiting my grandmother in Italy always felt so familiar to me—the same aromas, ingredients, and methods used in our home in the United States had origins on my grandmother's stove. My mother carried all of it in her head and heart when she left her homeland for a better life abroad. These recipes were her heirlooms.

It's no surprise that I felt that cooking has always been in my blood, and when I got older, I became a professional chef and recipe tester. After graduating from the French Culinary Institute, I could expertly julienne a carrot, bake a perfect soufflé, and work the line during a slammed dinner service without breaking a sweat. My interest in the origins of food led to my focus on food media, and I began working in test kitchens for any media outlet that would hire me. I became immersed in writing, testing, and perfecting recipes.

It wasn't until one day, not so long ago, while I was standing in my mom's basement watching her make meatballs, that a light bulb went off: *Why do I not know how to make my mom's meatballs?* She has made them countless times throughout my life—my grandmother in Italy made them before her—and yet, I had no idea about the spice blend, number of eggs, or how many cups of bread crumbs were needed. It hit me that despite all of my work in professional kitchens and all of the time I'd spent documenting the recipes of others, I did not have a record of my own family's heritage dishes.

I decided in that moment that I needed to start writing down all of my mother's recipes, the ones she makes for us at our weekly Sunday night get togethers, all from memory. Preserving these recipes—for my family, for my children—would ensure a piece of my mother's heritage—my heritage—would remain alive for generations to come.

At first, my mother didn't understand the need. Always humble, she never felt her recipes were special or extraordinary in any way. They were just the means to keep her family healthy and well fed. But after spending so many nights together working to make sure every ingredient was correctly represented, she began to take immense pride in her recipe collection. Calling me in the morning to go over what we should cook next became a daily ritual. She directed with a spoon as I furiously wrote down every step, forcing her to stop and measure, using a timer to determine cook time so no detail would be forgotten. I became obsessed with getting every recipe perfect. The project not only became a special bonding experience for us, but I believe it made my mother realize how important her meals really are to our family. Through them,

she taught us who she is and where she came from without saying a word. We learned about our heritage through our stomachs.

My "Nonna's meatball" project was a success, and I dream of the day I can hand down my collection of cherished recipes to my children, satisfied that my grandmother's recipes from Calabria will never be lost or forgotten.

This life-changing experience got me thinking: How many other immigrants, who expertly cook for their families every night, store the recipes in their heads? Probably most! Without their creators ever needing to write them down, would the recipes from abroad be lost if no one took the time to watch and learn?

I decided to expand what I began to call my "Nonna" project into a broader experiment. I cautiously sent out an email to a specific group of

friends—children of immigrants—asking them if I could "borrow" their mothers and grandmothers for the day. Would they like their mother's recipes written down and saved? I offered up my recipe-testing skills as a way to learn true home-cooked international fare and also provide a special service to each of these families. I guaranteed all the recipes I learned would be documented for them to keep forever. I was floored by the response. Everyone was thrilled to participate.

My first stop was Greece, by way of Long Island, New York. My dear friend Kostas was adamant his mother needed to cook with me, so he made a list of all his favorite dishes and set up the appointment. I was nervous—would a stranger be willing to share her secrets, to spend a day in the kitchen explaining each step, pausing to let me take pictures, actually measuring each ingredient? Needless to say, the experience was amazing. Kanella "Nelly," Kostas's mother, embraced the project, and me, with open arms. She made delicious Greek dishes like spanakopita with homemade

My sister Luciana and me, helping our mother, Gina, in the kitchen (and getting to taste the brodo) in 1989.

phyllo dough and pastitsio with glee as I followed her around her kitchen, jotting down ingredients, hearing stories about the old country, and truly feeling as if I were a member of her family. She was so honored that someone was interested in learning to make these dishes. It was an incredible day and secured in me the confidence that this project would be a success.

I began traveling to homes all over the country to hear stories, learn delicious dishes, and meet dynamic women who never realized how important their food is to their families and to the culture at large. Korea, China, Poland, Lebanon—each country so different, yet each kitchen I entered was the same: full of generous women cheering on my project, thanking me for coming, and feeding me delicious food. And similarly, their food, though different in many ways, represented the same thing: a love for family, a pride for their homeland, and, most importantly, an intimate gesture of warmth and caring for the well-being of their children.

I walked out of each of these kitchens with sage advice, deep insight, and a widened perspective. While cooking with these women, they retold their stories of raising their families in a new land, the struggles and the life-changing decisions that led them to leave everything behind to come to the Land of Opportunity. Each woman has given me a few delicious dishes to add to my recipe index, but much more than that, their stories of how food translates to culture, and how culture becomes a directional force in our lives, will always remain with me.

My true hope is that anyone looking through this collection of recipes and stories will remember that true American food is the food of immigrants. It is an amalgamation of the diverse cultures, traditions, and flavors that traveled to our shores throughout the last few centuries. May these recipes remind you of your own mother or grandmother, and inspire you to try one or two. May they fill your home with the smells and tastes of the great women who traveled a long way, with very little, to build a life in America.

Whether you are Italian, Korean, Russian, or just consider yourself true-blue American, the recipes in this book will resonate with you because they are the epitome of the melting pot that is our vital American heritage. Each recipe reproduced here has become part of the fabric of American food culture and deserves to be made time and time again.

By cooking with my mother, I learned to understand my Italian-American heritage. By eating with my non-Italian friends, cooking with their moms, and hearing about their pursuit of the American Dream, I learned something else: We could all afford to discover our *American* heritage at the bottom of a mixing bowl.

My first passport from when I immigrated to the United States as a baby.

ABOUT THIS BOOK

◆

"The United States is a nation of immigrants, each ethnic group retaining customs, festivals, and food traditions with great pride and yet with a stamp that is unmistakably American."

—THELMA BARER-STEIN,

AUTHOR OF *YOU EAT WHAT YOU ARE: PEOPLE, CULTURE AND FOOD TRADITIONS*

THROUGH THE WRITING of this cookbook, I have always had one very important aim: to inspire. I want the delicious recipes in this cookbook to inspire you to get into the kitchen, but I also want you to be inspired *by* these strong, empowering women and their beautiful stories.

Within you'll find many fascinating stories of immigration to the United States. Each one of these women will tell you how America truly is a Land of Opportunity, that when the prospect to leave their land of origin came, they knew their lives would be forever changed for the better. Democracy, freedom, and the ability to work hard for a better life were no longer the narratives of their dreams. Instead, they became an attainable reality they could grab onto for themselves and, most importantly, for their children.

Upon arrival, they each embraced the American way of life. They raised sons and daughters; many attended university, juggled work, learned English, and became citizens. But through it all, they maintained another critical practice: They held fast to their native culture. While encouraging their children to excel in school, they also made sure their mother tongue was spoken at home. Many became adventurous in the kitchen by learning how to roast a turkey for an American Thanksgiving, but they also incorporated the foods of their homeland into the holiday table and the nightly meals the family ate.

Maintaining the culture of their origin countries was not a statement; it simply created the comfort of home in a new place. Each day, heading out, speaking with an accent, and navigating this new world all became a little less overwhelming when the knowledge of a warm bowl of their own mother's food was waiting in the safe haven of their home. In their American kitchen, the swirling aromas of their country's ingredients and spice blends could be created within minutes of stepping through the door. That is the magic of food—it transports.

Immigrant women are a special group. Many speak with an accent, but do not underestimate them: The strength they showed at a young age, packing a bag, waving goodbye to their parents, and heading to a new and strange country was an epic feat. Their gumption and courage were boundless, and that fire still burns within them. Today, women from all over the world still see America as a place where life can be better, with more opportunities for themselves and their children.

So when you look around the food landscape of the United States, there is an undisputable fact: While these women may have jumped into our melting pot, they held their own spoons. As Tina Yao (page 112) said so eloquently, "People refer to the USA as a melting pot, but I'm not so sure. Instead, I think America is more of a stained-glass window. We come here, live, but we still remain who we are."

We do all come together, assimilate, and fit in to make the overall culture work and blend. However, each one of us also chose to maintain our pane of glass, which remains intact and shines bright among all the others.

Each woman featured in this book taught their families that they could be American *and* foreign, simultaneously. I hope you'll see this book as a testament to empowerment and strength, perseverance and inclusivity, and a warm and inspiring reminder that the story of immigrant food is, at its core, a story of American food. This, my friends, is what makes America great.

A NOTE ABOUT THE
RECIPES IN THIS BOOK

- The recipes in this book are my contributors' recipes, as remembered and shared by them. The beauty of food is that it can always be customized to suit your own tastes. Different regions, different cities, and even different chefs can have their own take on "authentic" recipes, and many recipes in this book have evolved to suit each individual woman's family's preferences over the years. Living in America also contributed to modifications to the recipes—there were times an ingredient wasn't available, or someone realized they really liked the taste of ketchup!

- If you see a recipe and think "that's not how my mother makes it," that's okay! If nothing else, I hope these recipes are a starting point for exploring more about each of the cultures represented and their foods. I also hope the recipes and women's stories spark cherished memories and conversation between you and your loved ones around your own heritage, culinary or otherwise.

- It was my desire to represent as many different countries and cuisines as possible. But the United States is so rich in diversity (and books, unfortunately, have a set number of pages), so this book represents only but a sampling of the cultures found in the United States.

"I only cook Greek food, my food. My children and grandchildren eat my food every day."

—KANELLA "NELLY" CHELIOTIS

Europe

Acri, Italy

GINA CROCCO
FRANCESE

◆

Gina Crocco Francese, my mother, grew up on a quiet countryside in southern Italy with her parents and five sisters.

NEARLY EVERYTHING SHE ATE AS a child came from her family's property. Whether it was potatoes, peas, wheat that was then turned into hand-cut pasta or fresh bread that was baked in the large outdoor hearth near their front door, or wine produced by their small vineyard, their sustainable Mediterranean diet was not only a source of food but a way of life.

As a child, Gina attended school and valued her studies, but she was also expected to help her mother and sisters tend to their crops, livestock, and large garden. In addition to the food they harvested on their own, delicious porcini mushrooms and wild strawberries grew in the woods nearby and so, whenever possible, she and her sisters would sell what they foraged to supplement the family's income. Gina learned from a young age that she had to work hard in order to thrive, because hard work very directly translated into food on the table.

Gina maintained this fierce work ethic, tenacity, and drive to succeed into her adulthood when she married and moved to the United States with her husband, Joseph, and young family. From the moment she arrived, she always had a job and never missed a day's work. Working hard mattered to her; it was a part of her identity, and she needed to prove to herself that she was equal to her American-born coworkers, despite needing to overcome a language barrier. She religiously attended her ESL classes, studied to get her driver's license, and felt extreme pride when she passed her citizenship test.

Whenever I visited her at work, people would gush about how critical her contribution was to whatever company she was working for at the time. She taught us to always take pride in what you do—no shortcuts, no easy ways out—and to make sure each day's work is exceptional. Economics dictated against Gina getting an education equal to her intellect, and even though she thrived in her own way, she felt it was especially important for my sister, Luciana, and me to work hard, excel in our studies, and live up to our potential. She was proud when grades came out and we were at the top of the class, and ecstatic when she saw we could lead our peers with determination and respect.

I have always taken for granted how difficult it must have been for my mother to leave behind her family, friends, and everything she knew for the chance at a better life for us. But despite being in a new place, she never forgot where she came from. After a hard day's work, she would come home and begin cooking the foods of her mother and grandmother for our young family. Whether it was her mother's cherished meatballs, a lasagna made from scratch, or a big pot of tomato sauce bubbling on the stove, Gina put food at the center of her home and family life. When I came through the door after school with my heavy backpack slung over my shoulder, I would find her in the kitchen rolling out the dough for pasta or mixing up the previous evening's risotto into arancini for a pre-dinner snack. If you closed your eyes and breathed deeply, as I often did, you wouldn't know if you were in our home or my grandparents' home: the smells were exactly the same.

Italy was an ocean away, but through my mother's cooking, it always seemed much closer than that to me. When we visited my grandparents as children or even now, when I am lucky enough to return, I feel like I am going home. The immigrant home carries with it the traditions, food, and heritage of the land our parents left behind. My mother's cooking proves that we are, quite literally, what we eat.

Gina's Arancini
(RICE BALLS)

serves — 8 (MAKES ABOUT 16 BALLS) | *PREP* 20 MINUTES | *TOTAL* 1 HOUR AND 10 MINUTES

GROWING UP IN a typical Southern Italian home, we didn't eat a lot of rice. We preferred pasta, and my mother served it regularly as our staple carbohydrate. Once in a while, however, my mom would whip up a risotto, and I would pout through dinner, pushing it to the edges of my plate hoping my father would think I had eaten some.

My very special consolation prize was the dish made the second day with plenty of leftover risotto (thanks to me): rice balls. When I throw a party, my mother always arrives with a big platter of arancini, so they have gained a bit of a cult following amongst my friends. My mother learned this rice ball recipe from her sister, Maria, who still lives in Calabria.

2 cups (380 g) Arborio rice

5 cups (1.2 L) chicken broth or water

½ tablespoon unsalted butter

1½ teaspoons extra-virgin olive oil

½ cup (80g) finely chopped prosciutto

1½ cups (150 g) Italian bread crumbs (Gina uses Progresso)

1 large egg, beaten

1 teaspoon parsley, chopped

⅓ cup (30 g) grated Parmigiano cheese

1 teaspoon coarse salt

4 ounces (115 g) fresh mozzarella, cut into ¼-inch (6-mm) cubes

4 cups (960 ml) vegetable oil

Grated parmesan cheese, for garnish

1. Combine the rice and broth in a large pot. Bring to a boil and then reduce to a simmer, cover, and cook until the water is absorbed and the rice is soft and creamy, about 15 to 20 minutes. Stir occasionally to ensure the rice doesn't stick to the bottom of the pot.

2. While the rice is cooking, heat the butter and olive oil in a small pan over medium heat and add the prosciutto. Cook until it begins to crisp, about 2 minutes. Set aside.

3. Once the rice is cooked, remove to a large baking sheet and let cool for 10 minutes. (Rice can be made a day ahead, cooled, and stored in the refrigerator overnight.)

4. While the rice is cooling, pour ½ cup (120 ml) room-temperature water into a shallow bowl. Place the bread crumbs in a separate shallow bowl. Set both aside.

5. Once the rice is cool, combine it with the crisped prosciutto, egg, parsley, Parmigiano cheese, and salt in a large bowl.

6. Using an ice cream scoop or lightly wet hands, create a 2-inch (5-cm) round ball with the rice mixture. Make an indentation in the middle and add a cube of mozzarella cheese. Encase the cheese with rice and reshape into a perfect ball, then set on the baking sheet. Repeat with the remaining rice mixture.

Gina, her mother, Grazia, and sister, Anna, in front of the family's outdoor hearth in Acri.

7. Using your hands, lightly wet the outside of each of the rice balls with the room-temperature water, then roll in the bread crumbs. Set them on the baking sheet.

8. Heat the vegetable oil in a large pot to 350°F (175°C). Drop 4 rice balls into the oil (they should fully submerge) and cook until the outside is golden brown, about 3 minutes. If your pot is wide, carefully roll the rice balls in the oil to ensure even cooking on all sides.

9. Transfer to paper towels to drain. Repeat with the remaining rice balls. They are best eaten at room temperature, garnished with a sprinkling of grated parmesan cheese, if you can wait!

GINA CROCCO FRANCESE

Gina's Tagliatelle

serves 4 TO 6 AS A FIRST COURSE | **PREP** 20 MINUTES | **TOTAL** 40 MINUTES

IN ITALY, MY grandmother never purchased pasta at the market; pasta was always made from scratch. I vividly remember the first time I saw her make hand-cut pasta, kneading the dough with strength and purpose until the scraggly pieces turned into a smooth and perfectly round ball. Then, after rolling it out and folding it up, she cut the dough into strips with her knife so quickly, the sound of the knife hitting the board was unforgettable. I love watching my mother make this recipe because it always brings me back to that special day in my grandmother's kitchen. The best part about my grandmother and mother's tagliatelle is that you don't need a mixer, fancy pasta maker, or even a bowl. All you need is a clean surface, a fork, a rolling pin, and a sharp knife.

4 cups (500 g) all-purpose flour, plus more for dusting

4 large eggs

1 tablespoon extra-virgin olive oil

1 cup (240 ml) warm water

1 teaspoon coarse salt

1. Pile the flour on a clean work surface or in a large wide bowl. Create a well in the middle and crack the eggs inside. Add the olive oil, water, and salt to the eggs and mix with a fork.

2. Slowly incorporate the flour as you mix. Once you have incorporated most of the flour, use both hands to create a ball of dough.

3. Knead the dough until it forms a smooth ball, 8 to 10 minutes. When you press into the dough with your thumb, it should bounce back. Separate the dough into 4 small balls and cover with a damp paper towel.

4. Flour a baking sheet and set aside.

5. Roll out one ball into a long, thin sheet with a rolling pin to about 14 × 9 inches (35.5 × 23 cm). Roll the dough around the rolling pin, then slide the rolling pin out. It will flatten into a rectangle. The dough will be thin but hearty (about ⅛ inch).

6. Starting at one end, cut thin strips (about ⅛ inch/3 mm wide) with a very sharp knife all the way through the dough. When you unroll the cut pieces you will have strips of dough that resemble fettuccine. Once you have cut all the strands, with floured hands, loosely arrange them in nests on the floured baking sheet until you are ready to cook. Repeat with the remaining dough balls.

7. Heat a large pot of water to a rolling boil. Place all of the cut pasta into the water and cook until al dente, about 8 to 10 minutes. Drain and dress with Brodo di Mamma e Polpette (page 25).

Nonna Gina cuts her pasta dough by hand just like her mother, Grazia, did back in Calabria.

GINA CROCCO FRANCESE

20

EUROPE | *Acri, Italy*

Gina's Bocconotti Calabrese
(ITALIAN HAND PIES)

makes 16 | PREP 25 MINUTES | TOTAL 40 MINUTES

MY MOTHER HAS never been much of a baker, but one dessert we enjoyed often was *bocconotti*. Bocconotti, which means "small bite" in Italian, is a pastry tartlet made with a sweet orange-scented dough filled with jam or chocolate. My mother still has tartlet forms from many years ago, but they can also be made in a traditional muffin tin. The tartlet forms create a beautiful fluted edge, so I prefer to bake them the traditional way. Bocconotti can be found all over Southern Italy, and my Calabrese family makes them for birthdays and holidays with homemade jam. My sister and I always preferred when my mom made them with Nutella, but she often forgot to separate them, so you had to say a quick prayer before you took a bite and hope that you'd find chocolate-hazelnut filling inside!

4 cups (500 g) all-purpose flour

1 cup (200 g) sugar

1 envelope (16 g) lievito vanigliato (vanilla-flavored yeast) (Gina uses Bertolini)

1 envelope (3 g) or 1 teaspoon vanilla powder (Gina uses Paneangeli Vanillina)

1¼ cups (256 g) vegetable shortening, plus more for pans

5 large eggs

Zest of 1 orange

2 teaspoons triple sec

1 cup (240 ml) chocolate-hazelnut spread (make Lisetta's Chocolate-Hazelnut Spread, page 31) or 1 cup (240 ml) cherry jam

Confectioners' sugar, for dusting

1. Preheat the oven to 350°F (175°C).

2. Sift the flour and sugar into a large bowl. Add the lievito vanigliato and vanilla powder and whisk to combine.

3. Add the shortening, 4 of the eggs, and the orange zest and knead until a shaggy dough forms.

4. Add the triple sec and continue to knead until a smooth ball of dough forms, 5 to 7 minutes.

5. Cover the dough with a tea towel and let it rest for 10 to 15 minutes.

6. Generously grease 1 to 2 tartlet forms or muffin pans with shortening (enough to accommodate 16).

7. Pinch off a 1½-inch (about 2-tablespoon) piece of dough and roll it into a ball. Flatten the ball on the counter, then place it into a tartlet form. Use your fingers to press it into the bottom and up the sides. Repeat 15 more times.

8. Place 1 tablespoon of the chocolate-hazelnut spread or jam into the middle of each piece of dough.

9. Pinch off another 1½-inch piece of dough, roll it into a ball, and flatten on the counter. Place it on top of one of the forms and pinch the edges together to seal in the filling. Repeat for the remaining forms.

10. Whisk the remaining egg with a bit of water, then brush the top of each bocconotti with a bit of the egg wash. Bake for 15 to 17 minutes, until the tops are golden brown.

11. Cool completely, then sprinkle with confectioners' sugar to serve.

Gina's Brodo di Mamma e Polpette

(MEATBALLS WITH TOMATO SAUCE)

serves 6 TO 8 | **PREP** 45 MINUTES | **TOTAL** 2 HOURS AND 25 MINUTES

ITALIAN GRANDMOTHERS ARE judged on the deliciousness of their meatballs and sauce, and every Italian insists his or her mother makes the ultimate meatball. Living in New York City for a good portion of my adult life, I have tried many meatballs. However, although many have tried to prove me wrong, I can safely say mamma Gina's are simply the best.

You must make the sauce for the meatballs first, because unlike some nonnas, my mother never fries or bakes her meatballs. Instead, they are cooked to perfection by simply poaching them in the sauce. Another secret? She uses her delicious sauce as an ingredient in the meatballs for juicy and delicious results Every. Single. Time!

FOR THE SAUCE (*BRODO DI MAMMA*)

10 fresh basil leaves

½ cup (120 ml) extra-virgin olive oil

2 garlic cloves, peeled and lightly smashed

2 teaspoons crushed red pepper (optional)

8 cups (2 L/two 32-ounce cans) crushed tomatoes

2 tablespoons tomato paste

1 tablespoon coarse salt

1 teaspoon freshly ground black pepper

FOR THE MEATBALLS (*POLPETTE*)

½ pound (227 g) ground pork

½ pound (227 g) ground veal

½ pound (227 g) ground chuck beef (85 percent lean)

1 tablespoon chopped parsley

1 tablespoon coarse salt

1 teaspoon freshly ground black pepper

2 large eggs, beaten

1 cup (100 g) freshly grated pecorino Romano cheese

1 cup (100 g) bread crumbs, preferably seasoned Italian (Gina uses Progresso)

½ cup (120 ml) whole milk

½ cup (120 ml) *Brodo di Mamma*, cooled

1. ***Make the sauce.*** Tear 5 of the basil leaves in half; reserve the rest. Combine the torn basil, olive oil, garlic, and crushed red pepper, if using, in a small pan and heat over very low heat, allowing the basil and garlic to "steep" in the olive oil for 10 to 15 minutes. The oil will become fragrant and rich with flavor—be careful to not let the garlic burn or go beyond a medium-brown color. Remove from the heat, strain the aromatics, and set the oil aside.

Continues

2. Combine the crushed tomatoes and 2 cups (480 ml) of water in a large pot. Add the tomato paste, salt, and pepper. Pour in the infused oil and stir to combine. Bring to a boil over medium-high heat, then immediately reduce to a simmer. Remove ½ cup (120 ml) of the brodo for the meatballs, setting aside to cool.

3. Partially cover the pot and simmer for 1 hour.

4. ***Make the meatballs.*** In a large bowl, hand-mix all the meatball ingredients. (This prevents overmixing.) The mixture will be very soft, but resist the urge to add more bread crumbs; you're making tender, melt-in-your-mouth meatballs. Once all the ingredients are combined, wet your hands and pinch off a golf-ball sized piece of the mixture (about ¼ cup) and roll it into a ball. Place each meatball on a baking sheet and repeat with the remaining mixture, making approximately 16 to 18 meatballs.

5. Carefully drop the meatballs into the sauce. If the pot seems too full, shimmy the pot back and forth to make more room. (Do not stir with a spoon—you will break the meatballs!)

6. Simmer the meatballs in the sauce for 45 minutes or up to 2 hours. The longer it cooks, the better it tastes. Carefully remove the meatballs to a plate. Chop the remaining basil and sprinkle on top of the sauce. Serve with Tagliatelle (page 20) or the pasta of your choice.

Note

Mamma Gina's meatballs freeze exceptionally well. After step 4, freeze directly on the baking sheet, then transfer to freezer bags once fully frozen. They will keep up to a month. When ready to cook, make Mamma's brodo and drop the frozen meatballs right into the sauce. Cook for 1 to 2 hours.

MARIETTA "MARIA" MIRAFIORE

◆

MARIA NEVER INTENDED TO LEAVE the lovely little town of San Lucido where she was raised. Even after her parents immigrated to the United States, she was content remaining in her hometown with her growing family. However, while she was pregnant with her fifth child, tragedy unexpectedly struck, and her husband, Dante, died suddenly. Although she wasn't sure she wanted to leave, her parents urged her to join them in America.

So she boarded a plane with the resolution to start over, to raise her young children as Americans. At first, she moved in with her parents, but she immediately found work and began saving with the intention of venturing out on her own. Because of her tireless work ethic and long hours at a local hospital, after five years she was able to buy a home and move her family into a place of their own.

As her children grew, she continued to work and support them by herself—her parents assisted and provided guidance, but she never remarried. Now that they are grown, she is the loving head of her large family and spends many hours cooking for and looking after her grandchildren. She was also always willing to work hours at her son Robert's pizzeria, an enterprise that made use of many of her family's recipes from their homeland.

Maria loves tending her garden, which is filled with peppers, tomatoes, and other delicious vegetables that she cans and stores for winter. At family dinners, she gets requests for many of her traditional Italian dishes, but her eggplant patties (page 28) and stuffed vinegar peppers (page 29) are Mirafiore family favorites. Ever the strong matriarch, Maria cites her children as her best achievements—their accomplishments are her accomplishments—and she's still proud of how she came here, worked hard, and lived the American dream all on her own.

Maria's Eggplant Patties

THESE LITTLE PATTIES are a favorite of Maria's children and grandchildren. They are so tasty and savory, you would think they had meat in them (but they don't!). For a healthier version, Maria bakes them, but the fried version is the one the family craves. She makes hers a small appetizer size, but be careful—you will lose count of how many you eat!

3 large eggplants, peeled and quartered

6 garlic cloves, minced

3 tablespoons parsley, chopped fine

1½ cups (150 g) bread crumbs

¾ cup (75 g) grated Parmigiano cheese

3 large eggs, beaten

2 teaspoons coarse salt

2 teaspoons freshly ground black pepper

1 cup (240 ml) canola oil or light olive oil

1. Bring 10 cups (2.4 L) water to a boil in a large stock pot.

2. Add the eggplant and press to submerge. Boil until the eggplant is fork-tender, 10 to 12 minutes.

3. Drain the eggplant in a colander. Then, place in a large bowl and add cold water to cool. Drain the water again and squeeze each piece to remove excess water.

4. Mince the eggplant until it becomes a pulp.

5. Combine the eggplant pulp, garlic, parsley, bread crumbs, cheese, eggs, salt, and pepper in a large bowl with your hands until fully incorporated.

6. Heat ¼ cup (60 ml) canola oil in a large cast-iron skillet over medium heat.

7. Form small balls (about the size of a golf ball) of the eggplant mixture and then flatten them with your hand before placing them in the skillet.

8. Cook for 6 to 7 minutes on each side to form a golden-brown crust. Repeat with any remaining mixture, adding more oil as needed.

9. Transfer to a serving platter. Serve warm or at room temperature.

In August of 1972, Maria boarded a plane for America with her five children: Roberto, Bruno, Rosa, Antonella, and Daniella.

Maria's Stuffed Vinegar Peppers

serves 5 (MAKES 15 STUFFED PEPPERS) | **PREP** 20 MINUTES, PLUS PICKLING | **TOTAL** 1 HOUR AND 20 MINUTES

THE MIRAFIORE FAMILY gets very excited when Maria makes these peppers. They are a true labor of love. First, she grows rows and rows of Hungarian wax peppers each summer. Then, after the harvest, she pickles them. Finally, after a few months in the brine, she stuffs and bakes them for a spicy appetizer with a bit of a vinegar kick. Delicious! Her grandson Dante, chef and owner of Dante's Pizza in New Canaan, Connecticut (like her son Robert, pizzaiolos run in the family!), is impatient, so sometimes he does a quick pickle of the peppers before proceeding with the recipe, but even he admits his aren't as good as Nonna's.

FOR THE VINEGAR PEPPERS
15 large Hungarian wax peppers or cubanelle peppers

1 cup (240 ml) white vinegar

1 teaspoon coarse salt

FOR THE STUFFING
1 teaspoon plus 2 tablespoons extra-virgin olive oil

8 ounces (227 g) spicy pork sausage, casing removed

2 cups (75 g) Italian bread torn into small pieces

1 large egg, beaten

1 garlic clove, minced

½ cup (50 g) grated pecorino Romano cheese

2 tablespoons Italian parsley, chopped

1. *Prepare the vinegar peppers.* Place the peppers in a large glass mason jar. Add the vinegar, 1½ cups (360 ml) water, and the salt and close the jar very tightly. Set it aside and allow the peppers to pickle for at least 2 months.

2. *Make the stuffed peppers.* Remove the peppers from the brine, reserving the brine.

3. Heat 1 teaspoon of the extra-virgin olive oil in a large sauté pan over medium heat.

4. Add the sausage, breaking it up with a wooden spoon, until cooked through, 6 to 7 minutes. Transfer the cooked sausage to a large bowl.

5. While the sausage cooks, place the bread in a small bowl and add just enough reserved brine to cover. Let soak for 2 to 3 minutes.

6. Combine the bread and the sausage, then add the egg, garlic, cheese, and parsley. Mix to combine.

7. Preheat the oven to 375°F (190°C).

8. Remove the stem end of a pepper, then clip the tip to allow steam to escape.

9. Fill the pepper with the stuffing, using your fingers to push the stuffing as far into the tip as you can.

10. Place the stuffed peppers on a baking sheet and drizzle with the remaining 2 tablespoons olive oil.

11. Bake for 45 minutes to 1 hour. The peppers are done once they are charred and the stuffing begins to pop out of the pepper.

12. To serve, gently push the stuffing back in and place the peppers on a serving platter.

MARIETTA MIRAFIORE

EUROPE | *San Lucido, Italy*

LISETTA FARRIS

◆

GROWING UP IN BOTH ROME and Florence, Lisetta learned the value of good food, beautiful art, and a rich culture at a very young age. Although she had an exciting urban upbringing, she spent her summers running free in the fields of her grandparents' large property and vineyard in Sardinia. She remembers, quite fondly, how her grandparents taught her about farm life: getting up early, hunting rabbit for dinner, and learning how the soil helped produce the delicious foods her grandmother, Margherita, would cook every night.

An eager apprentice, Lisetta learned how to butcher chickens and rabbits, make homemade pasta, and, most importantly, how to bargain with the fruit vendors for the freshest produce at even better prices. Her grandmother instilled in her the value of cooking food for the pure pleasure of it. The goal of a good meal should be to please your family and to show your love through the flavors of the food. When Lisetta cooks today for her husband, Andrea, and children, Alessandro and Carolina, she tries to replicate the flavors of her grandmother's kitchen—the flavors of her carefree summer days, spending time with her loving family.

Lisetta's Chocolate - Hazelnut Spread

makes APPROXIMATELY 3 CUPS (720 ML) | **PREP** 15 MINUTES | **TOTAL** 25 MINUTES

ONCE YOU MAKE this easy, five-ingredient Nutella-like spread, you might never buy the jarred variety again! If you want to eat it like an Italian, generously slather it on some crusty bread for a delicious snack. It is also a fantastic filling for Gina's Bocconotti (page 23). Store any leftovers in the fridge, but let it come to room temperature before eating for better spreadability.

1½ cups (205 g) hazelnuts (Lisetta prefers Piedmonte hazelnuts)

½ cup (100 g) granulated sugar

6 ounces (170 g) high-quality milk chocolate

6 ounces (170 g) high-quality dark chocolate, at least 70 percent cocoa

1 cup (240 ml) whole milk

2 tablespoons hazelnut oil

1. Preheat the oven to 350°F (175°C).

2. Place the hazelnuts on a baking sheet and toast in the oven until fragrant and golden brown, 7 to 8 minutes.

3. While the hazelnuts are toasting, combine the sugar, chocolate, and milk in a small saucepan over low heat until the chocolate has completely melted.

4. Let the toasted hazelnuts cool for ten minutes. Add them to a food processor and grind until they turn into a paste, similar to a nut butter.

5. Add the chocolate mixture to the food processor and process, gradually adding the hazelnut oil. Continue to process all the ingredients until fully combined.

6. Store in an airtight container in the refrigerator for up to 1 week.

LISETTA FARRIS

Lisetta's Coniglio Alla Garda

(SARDINIAN RABBIT)

serves 4 TO 6 | *PREP* 10 MINUTES | *TOTAL* 45 MINUTES

LISETTA WAS FORTUNATE to be surrounded by talented cooks on both sides of her family. This recipe was given to Lisetta by her other loving grandmother, Carolina. Lisetta remembers how her grandfather would go out early in the morning to catch the hare for supper. He taught Lisetta the trick to catching a quick-moving rabbit: When quietly approaching him, make sure the sun is NOT at your back, otherwise the smart little rabbit will see your shadow and jump away before you can grab it. Yes, grab it—Lisetta's grandfather would grab them by the ears with his own two hands!

This dish is perfect as a second course, or as Italians call it, *il secondo*. This recipe is simple and quick but has a delicious flavor imparted from the lean rabbit and briny capers. The sauce will reduce down to a delicious glaze that makes even the smallest pieces finger-licking good! I love to serve it with a basket of fresh-cut Italian bread to sop up the sauce.

1 (2-pound/907 g) rabbit, washed and trimmed of all excess fat (see Note)

¼ cup plus 2 tablespoons (90 ml) extra-virgin olive oil

4 garlic cloves

4 bay leaves

2 teaspoons coarse salt

1 teaspoon freshly ground black pepper

½ cup (120 ml) dry white wine

¼ cup (60 ml) white wine vinegar

2 tablespoons capers, drained and rinsed

3 tablespoons tomato paste

1. Thoroughly wash the rabbit and dry with paper towels. Cut it into six pieces, through the joints. Set aside.

2. Heat the olive oil with 3 garlic cloves in a large sauté pan over medium heat for 3 minutes.

3. Add the rabbit pieces and bay leaves, and brown the meat for 5 minutes. Remove the garlic.

4. Flip the rabbit pieces and cook for 5 more minutes. Add the salt and pepper.

5. Add the wine, vinegar, and capers and simmer for 3 minutes. The meat should release from the pan.

6. Add the tomato paste and the remaining clove of garlic. With a wooden spoon, carefully mix the paste into the pan sauce, turning the meat to cover with the liquid.

7. Pour ½ cup (120 ml) water into the pan, reduce the heat to low, and cover. Simmer for 10 to 12 minutes.

8. Remove the lid and check the dish: It is done when the oil begins to separate and the sauce is a deep red color.

Note If you'd like, you can substitute the rabbit with one 2-pound (907 g) whole chicken, cut into 8 pieces. Just adjust the cook time to 40 minutes in step 7.

Europe

Bila Tserkva, Ukraine (Former USSR)

EMILYA "EMILY" AYZENBERG KAPLAN

Emily always dreamed of a better life.

ALTHOUGH SHE WAS BORN AND raised in the Ukraine, she never truly felt at home. The Ukraine was a place of religious strife for many Jewish families, even though they spoke the same language, went to the same schools, and worked side by side with Ukrainians of other religions. At the time, being Jewish was simply not accepted, and those who tried to honor their culture were punished: The authorities made it impossible for Jewish people to worship freely, and Emily knew that no matter how hard she studied, very few Jewish students were accepted to university.

In addition, Emily was raised in a single-parent home with a very limited income. Every day was a struggle, as, at the time, there was no government assistance for single mothers or the poor. Despite her disadvantages and the adversity she felt, she excelled in school, beating the odds, and was accepted to university, where she studied electrical engineering and met and married her husband, Isyaslav ("Isaac"). They soon had two daughters, Irina and Olga. After she completed school, she was more anxious than ever to start anew in a different place.

With the political tide turning, Emily and her husband saw their chance at a new life, and they were desperate to take it. After a long wait, in 1988, permission to leave the USSR was granted. They were issued visas to Israel for themselves, their children, and her mother, Eva. Emily remembers that time well: "We were stateless, had no money, didn't know the language, my mother's health was failing, and yet, we were so happy!"

Along with thousands of other Jewish families, they left everything behind and headed to Austria. Vienna became an arrival station for many migrants and refugees of many nations. With their Israeli visas in hand, the Kaplans could depart for Israel straightaway. However, while they felt Israel was a safe haven for Jews, the Kaplans believed America was the land of opportunity, a place where their dreams would be realized. They surrendered the Israeli visas and headed to the US embassy to apply for visas.

With so many people holding fast to the same dream, they were told America could not absorb all of the immigrants, and Emily's family received a refusal. Crushed at the news, Emily's mother reminded her *We never give up*—so they forged ahead. Embarking for Italy instead, they maintained hope for a US entrance visa. Once in Rome, they immediately applied again and waited for an answer.

Italy proved hard. While many Jewish charity organizations were working to provide refugees with food, shelter, and money, the number of refugees from Russia was too great and there wasn't enough assistance to go around. With no money or guarantee of a visa, they lived in an abandoned beach town with little food and no heat. Hope dwindled.

Finally, after three months, they were granted passage to the United States, and they arrived in New York City. They received a three-month stay in a hotel to get themselves settled. Penniless and facing imminent eviction, they set out to earn enough money to find permanent lodging. As her husband had predicted, America was full of opportunities, and he found work immediately. Emily, with her determination and fierce work ethic, also worked twelve-hour days, seven days a week cleaning homes.

In those three short months, they saved enough to rent and furnish an apartment. They lived there for five years before buying a home in Sheepshead Bay, Brooklyn, the neighborhood that they reside in to this day. Emily learned to read and write English by translating her daughter Olga's first-grade homework assignments from English to Russian, so her daughter could keep up at school. She took accounting and computer courses and maintained a career while raising her girls.

Emily's mother was a strong woman who not only taught Emily to cook, but instilled in her a sense of hope and a will to work hard for a better future. The meals they cooked together when she was a young woman in the Ukraine are the same dishes Emily still cooks for her family today. Like many women who learned to cook by rote, Emily does not use measuring equipment or written recipes. Her recipes have been passed down from generation to generation. Now, her two daughters honor these recipes of the past and prepare them for their children as well.

EMILY'S UKRAINIAN
Deviled or "Stuffed" Eggs

serves 6 TO 8 AS A STARTER | **PREP** 20 MINUTES | **TOTAL** 20 MINUTES

THIS DISH IS traditionally served to guests before dinner. Emily stuffs them high and then rounds off the filling. Unlike the deviled eggs common at summer picnics, there is no mayonnaise in the traditional Ukrainian recipe. Instead, the filling gets a punch of flavor from crispy onions and carrots. But when Emily's girls come to visit, she makes two versions: the traditional one and then another batch with a bit of mayonnaise added because Emily's daughter Irina prefers hers with a creamier filling. So, if that is your preference as well, add 1 teaspoon of mayonnaise to the vegetables after they have cooled.

6 large eggs, hard-boiled

1 tablespoon neutral-flavored oil, such as canola or peanut

1 medium carrot, finely grated (about ½ cup/ 55 g)

1 small onion, finely chopped (about ¼ cup/ 30 g)

1 teaspoon coarse salt, or more to taste

1 tablespoon finely chopped fresh dill

1. Peel and halve the eggs lengthwise. Separate the yolks and place all but two of them into a medium bowl. Discard the remaining whole yolk (two halves).

2. Heat the oil in a small sauté pan over medium heat. Cook the carrot and onion until they begin to soften and turn a dark golden color, about 5 minutes. Set aside to cool slightly.

3. Add the cooked vegetables to the yolks and mash with a fork to create a paste. Season with the salt.

4. Spoon a heaping teaspoon of the filling into each egg half. Round off and garnish with the dill.

Emily purchased this meat grinder in Italy, which she used to process the turkey rations her family ate while there.

EMILYA AYZENBERG KAPLAN

EUROPE | *Bila Tserkva, Ukraine (Former USSR)*

Emily's Apple Blinchiki

(APPLE "PANCAKES")

serves 4 (MAKES 9 PANCAKES, APPROX. 2½ INCHES IN DIAMETER) | *PREP* 5 MINUTES | *TOTAL* 15 MINUTES

TRADITIONALLY, BLINCHIKI IS a simple crepe-like pancake. However, Emily's mother, Eva, always grated apples into the batter to make it a heartier dish. I never knew a four-ingredient recipe could taste so good! Emily makes these often for her grandchildren, and it's their favorite after-school snack. For a show-stopping breakfast or dessert, serve them with Emily's Sour Cherry Sauce (page 40).

2 apples, sweet or sour depending on preference (Emily prefers sweet, like Gala or Honeycrisp)

1 large egg, beaten

5 to 6 tablespoons (37 to 45 g) all-purpose flour

1 tablespoon sunflower oil or butter

Sour cream

Emily's Sour Cherry Sauce (page 40)

1. Peel and grate the apples on the large holes of a box grater.

2. Combine the grated apple with the egg in a large bowl.

3. Add the flour, 1 tablespoon at a time, until all the moisture is absorbed. The mixture will resemble chunky pancake batter.

4. Heat the sunflower oil in a large pan over medium heat. Spoon 3 to 4 small dollops of the batter onto the pan. Press them to create round, chunky pancakes. Cook until the center is firm and the outside is golden brown, 3 to 4 minutes per side.

5. Serve with sour cream and/or Sour Cherry Sauce (page 40).

EMILYA AYZENBERG KAPLAN

EUROPE | *Bila Tserkva, Ukraine (Former USSR)*

Emily's Sour Cherry Sauce

makes 3 CUPS (720 ML) | PREP 5 MINUTES | TOTAL 2½ HOURS

THIS SAUCE IS simple and delicious. As a child, Emily loved the flavor of the sweet cherries with her tea—she remembers how she would gulp a cherry or two down with the hot tea her mother would make her. This sauce is fantastic on Blinchiki (page 38), but a spoonful or two is great dolloped onto some vanilla ice cream, too.

5¼ cups (815 g) sour cherries, pitted   4 cups (800 g) sugar

1. Place the cherries in a large pot and pour the sugar on top. Shake the pot from side to side to mix, being careful to not break up the fruit.

2. Let the mixture to stand for 1 hour, shaking the pot every 20 minutes to evenly distribute the sugar. By the end of the hour, the sugar will be almost completely dissolved and the liquid will have pooled in the pot.

3. Cook the cherries over medium-low heat to dissolve any remaining sugar, about 5 minutes, shaking the pot occasionally to mix.

4. Increase the heat to medium-high and bring to a boil. Boil for about 5 minutes, skimming the white foam that rises to the top with a large spoon.

5. Reduce to a simmer and cook for 5 more minutes, shaking the pot occasionally.

6. Remove from the heat and cool to room temperature, about 25 minutes.

7. Once the mixture is cooled, return the pot to the stove and repeat steps 4 through 6 for a second time.

8. Once the mixture has cooled for a second time, return the pot to the stove and repeat steps 4 through 6 for a third time. When it is completely cooled, it will have a thin, syrupy consistency.

Europe

Chernovtsi, Ukraine (Former USSR)

TSILIA SORINA

◆

WHILE PATIENTLY WAITING FOR WORD that her family could leave the Ukraine in the early 1980s, Tsilia, a respected physician, was raising her two young boys, Alexander and Boris, tending her home, and practicing medicine. She had hopes for a new life, and she dreamed of leaving the Ukraine behind and starting over in America. She knew the future was uncertain—she would have to study for and retake her medical certifications to prove her abilities before she could practice medicine in her new home—but she felt that if her sons were to have a good life, she had to leave.

Weekly, her husband, Roman, would head to town to see if they had been granted permission to go. One fateful morning, Tsilia was busy in the kitchen packing herbs from her garden in salt (a task Ukrainian women take very seriously because it's important to have a store of fresh herbs to last the long winters). As she was completing this laborious process, her husband charged into the kitchen yelling, "We can go, we can go! Finally, our day has come to get out!" Her immediate response was surprising: "Well, then what am I going to do with all these herbs?!"

While this story has become a family tale that brings a laugh and a bit of levity to their past, it also shows this mother's love and commitment to nourishing her family. Although she felt excitement about the journey, she also felt a bit unsure and fearful about life in America: In addition to not knowing the language or where they would end up, she had no idea what kind of food they would find. She remembers feeling relief when they reached New York and she saw that the ingredients she needed for her family recipes were readily available. From then on, life would be different in many ways, but the family table would remain comfortingly the same.

Tsilia's Gefilte Fish

SERVES 8 TO 10 | **PREP** 20 MINUTES | **TOTAL** 3 HOURS AND 20 MINUTES, PLUS CHILLING

TSILIA'S PRESENTATION OF this dish is very unique. She has her fishmonger give her the head and tail from one of the fish, and she sets them on the platter with the gefilte fish in place of the body, making it look as if the fish swam right onto the table. Most people buy this traditional dish during the holidays, but Tsilia makes her own every year.

2 tablespoons vegetable oil

3 large onions, minced

2 to 3 pounds (907 g to 1.4 kg) ground fish from a combination of carp, white fish, and pike (see Note)

4 large eggs, beaten

Coarse salt

Freshly ground black pepper

2 tablespoons sugar

2 tablespoons (30 ml) club soda

¼ to ⅓ cup (25 to 35 g) plain bread crumbs

Sliced carrots

Parsley sprigs

Prepared horseradish

1. Heat the oil in a large pan over medium heat. Add the onions and sauté until softened but not brown, about 5 minutes. Set aside to cool.

2. Combine the ground fish, one-third of the cooked onions (about ¾ cup/90 g), the eggs, 2 teaspoons salt, 1 teaspoon pepper, 1 tablespoon of the sugar, the club soda, and ¼ cup (25 g) of the bread crumbs. Add another 1 to 2 tablespoons of bread crumbs if the mixture seems too loose. Set ½ cup of the mixture aside, or enough to fill the head of the fish.

3. Bring 8 to 10 cups (2 to 2.4 L) water to a boil.

4. Place the remaining cooked onions in the bottom of a large Dutch oven, wide stockpot, or fish poaching pan. Cut a 12 × 15-inch (30.5 × 38-cm) piece of parchment paper or cheesecloth and lay it on a flat surface. Place the fish mixture in the center and pat it into a 10 × 5-inch (25 × 12-cm) rectangle about 1 inch (2.5 cm) tall. Take the sides of the parchment or cheesecloth and fold them around the rectangle, creating a package to hold the shape. Secure the folds in place with a toothpick if you like.

Note

The best way to get this combination of fish is to visit a fishmonger. Have them remove the bones and head from 6 pounds (2.7 kg) whole fish and grind the fish for you (if you choose, you can also grind the fish at home). This will yield 2 to 3 pounds (907 g to 1.4 kg) ground fish. Ask to keep the head and tail from one of the fish to use for your final presentation.

TSILIA SORINA

5. Gently place the wrapped fish on top of the onions in the pot. Pour boiling water over the fish to cover (you will not need all of it; keep the remaining water at a boil to be used in step 6). Add the remaining tablespoon of sugar, 1 tablespoon salt, and 1 teaspoon pepper to the water. Bring to a gentle simmer and cook for 3½ to 4 hours, uncovered, until the fish is firm.

6. Meanwhile, rinse the fish head with cold water until it runs clear. Fill the fish head with the reserved fish mixture from step 2. Wrap the head and the tail together in parchment paper and place in a pot. Cover with boiling water and simmer for 1 to 1½ hours, until the fish mixture is firm.

7. When all the fish is done cooking, gently remove it from the pot and remove the parchment. Let it cool, then refrigerate for a few hours or overnight.

8. To serve, place the cooked fish rectangle in the center of large serving platter. Set the cooked head at one end and the tail at the other.

9. Garnish with carrots and parsley, and serve with horseradish on the side. It is best served cold or at room temperature.

◆

TSILIA SORINA

43

Tsilia's Borscht

(BEEF AND BEET STEW)

serves 6 TO 8 | **PREP** 15 MINUTES | *TOTAL* 5 HOURS

DEEP RED AND chock-full of beef and vegetables, this soup has gotten many through a cold winter night. Tsilia likes to squeeze some lemon in at the end to brighten the dish, and I love it with a swirl of sour cream.

2 to 3 pounds (907 g to 1.4 kg) stew beef, cut into 4-inch (10-cm) chunks

12-ounce bag (340g) lima beans, not organic

1 large onion, peeled

2 medium beets, peeled

1 medium carrot, peeled and grated

1 garlic clove

1 cubanelle pepper, seeded, one half grated

2 large potatoes (about 1 pound/455 g), peeled and quartered

1¼ cups (300 ml) tomato juice

1 small cabbage, finely chopped (about 8 cups/560 g)

1 bay leaf

3 tablespoons fresh dill

Coarse salt

Freshly ground black pepper

1 lemon

Sour cream

1. Bring 2 cups (480 ml) water to a boil in a large stockpot. Add the beef and cook for 10 minutes. Add more water, if necessary, to fully cover the beef. Drain, then rinse the beef. Return the beef to the pot and add 10 cups (2.4 L) of hot water. Simmer the beef over medium heat for 40 minutes, then add the lima beans (no need to soak). Reduce to a more gentle simmer and cook for 2 hours.

2. Add the onion and beets and about ½ cup (120 ml) hot water to ensure all the meat and vegetables remain covered. Simmer for another 30 minutes.

3. Remove the beef and set aside. Remove the beets, cut each in half, and place two of the halves back in the pot. Grate the remaining two halves and add to the pot. Add the carrot, garlic, and cubanelle pepper to the pot. Simmer for another 20 minutes.

4. Add the potatoes and tomato juice, cover, and simmer for another 30 minutes.

5. Add the beef back to the pot along with the cabbage and bay leaf. Cover and simmer for a final 30 minutes. Remove the bay leaf if you wish.

6. Add the dill, salt, and pepper to taste, and a squeeze of lemon to finish. Serve with a dollop of sour cream.

TSILIA SORINA

45

Tsilia's Siberian Pelmeni

(PORK AND BEEF DUMPLINGS)

Serves — 8 TO 10 (MAKES ABOUT 70 PELMENI) | **PREP** 15 MINUTES | **TOTAL** 1½ HOURS

THESE DELICIOUS LITTLE dumplings come together with only a handful of ingredients, but they still pack a lovely flavor. For serving, Tsilia puts the butter, ground pepper, and strong Russian vinegar right on the table, so each diner can add either a pat of butter, a bit of cracked pepper, or a splash of some vinegar (or all three!) on top of the hot pelmeni.

3 cups (375 g) all-purpose flour, plus more for rolling

Coarse salt

1 large egg

½ pound (227 g) 90% lean ground beef

½ pound (227 g) ground pork

1 small onion, finely chopped

Freshly ground black pepper

Unsalted butter, melted

White vinegar

1. Mix the flour with 1 teaspoon salt in a large bowl. Create a well in the center of the flour and crack the egg into the well. Using a fork, mix the egg and flour together. Add ¾ cup (180 ml) water and knead to make a dough. If it's too dry, add up to ¼ cup (60 ml) more water. If it's too wet, add up to ¼ cup (30 g) more flour. Turn the dough out onto a floured surface and knead by hand until smooth, 5 to 7 minutes. Place under a dish towel and set aside.

2. Combine the beef, pork, onion, 1 teaspoon salt, and 1 teaspoon pepper.

3. Cut the dough into 4 equal pieces. Keep 3 pieces under the towel and roll out the remaining piece to ⅛ inch (3 mm) thick.

4. Using a round 2-inch (5-cm) cutter, cut the dough into circles. Place 1 teaspoon of the filling in the middle of each circle. Fold the circle in half, enclosing the filling, and using wet fingers, seal the halves together. With the sealed edge facing up, bring the two bottom corners together at the bottom, and pinch and seal to create a small dumpling. Repeat with the remaining dough, re-rolling any leftover scraps.

5. Fill a large pot halfway with water and bring to a boil. Add 1 tablespoon salt.

6. Place half the pelmeni in the water and boil until the dough cooks through and they plump up and rise to the surface, about 5 minutes. Stir to ensure they aren't sticking to each other, reduce to a simmer, and cook for 2 more minutes. Remove the pelmeni with a slotted spoon and place on a serving dish. Repeat with the remaining pelmeni.

7. Serve with black pepper, melted butter, and/or white vinegar.

TSILIA SORINA

EUROPE | *Chernovtsi, Ukraine (Former USSR)*

MARINA VARSHISKY

IMMIGRATION WASN'T NEW TO MARINA Varshisky when she came to the United States as a young wife and mother. Picking up and moving to a better place had been a critical piece of her family's history for many generations. She recounted how her father, as a young boy, migrated to Siberia after narrowly escaping the German invasion of Kazakhstan. That fateful day changed the course of their lives and their future.

Although Kazakhstani by heritage, Marina grew up in Siberia with her parents and a grandmother who always taught her to be confident. If someone attempted to shame her for her gender or religion, at her grandmother's instruction she would always assert how proud she was of who she was. She remembers how those who taunted her quickly stopped bothering her once they knew she would not tolerate being bullied.

She focused on her studies and was accepted into medical school in Moscow, where she met her husband, Michael. They married and had two girls, Asya and Anna. Then, at twenty-nine years old, the opportunity to come to the United States presented itself, and they decided to leave Russia behind for a brighter future for themselves and their children. They moved, had another child, Samuel, and later reunited with her parents, Garry and Galina, who immigrated a few years after. They all still live close to each other today.

While cooking Marina's delicious, traditional food and speaking with her about her family, it is quite evident that the confidence she learned as a young girl has served her well. She came to the United States, built a beautiful life with her husband, and raised three successful children. Now she gets to dote on her two grandchildren as well. Love for family, love for her heritage, and the quest for a better life is simply a part of who she is, and with that comes all the pride and confidence one could ever hope for.

Marina's "Herring Under a Fur Coat"
(DRESSED-HERRING CASSEROLE)

serves 8 | **PREP** 45 MINUTES | **TOTAL** 50 MINUTES

THE FLAVOR COMBINATION in this cold, layered, dressed-herring casserole, a traditional appetizer for the New Year, might surprise you. The saltiness from the herring and the richness of the mayonnaise and sour cream with all those vegetables sandwiched in between doesn't seem as if it will work, but it does.

2 large potatoes
(about 1 pound/455 g)

6 large carrots, peeled, trimmed, and cut in half (about 6 oz. or 170 g each)

3 medium red beets
(about 6 oz. or 170 g each)

2 cups (480 ml) mayonnaise

1 cup (240 ml) sour cream

6 large Dutch herring, first catch

6 large eggs, hard-boiled and grated

1 large onion, cut in half and sliced into thin half-moons

1 cup (156 g) pomegranate seeds (optional)

1. Bring 5 cups of water to a boil in a large pot. Add the potatoes to the pot and boil for 2 minutes. Then, add the carrots and boil for another 6 to 8 minutes, until both the potatoes and the carrots are fork-tender. Remove from the pot and set aside to cool.

2. Add the beets to the same water and cook for 10 to 12 minutes, until fork-tender. Remove from the pot and set aside to cool.

3. When cool, peel the potatoes and beets. Grate each vegetable on the large holes of a box grater, keeping each vegetable separate.

4. Combine the mayonnaise and sour cream in a small bowl. Set aside.

5. Cut the herring into bite-size pieces and spread in a layer on the bottom of a casserole or trifle dish.

6. Lay half of the grated potato over the herring to create a second layer. Cover with half of the grated carrots, then half of the grated eggs, followed by half of the sliced onion and half of the grated beets.

7. Spread a thin layer of the mayonnaise mixture on top of the grated beets.

8. Repeat the layers using the remaining ingredients. The final layer should be the remainder of the mayonnaise mixture. Store in the fridge until you are ready to serve. Can be served cold or at room temperature.

9. Sprinkle pomegranate seeds on top, if desired, to serve.

This Russian cookbook, published in 1960, the year Marina was born, was given to her by her parents on her wedding day. After her father came to the United States, he had it rebound for her.

MARINA VARSHISKY

Marina's Poppy Seed Cake

MARINA STARTED MAKING this cake when she moved to Moscow for college. She began soaking the poppy seeds overnight because she found it softens them and improves their flavor. Make sure to buy fresh poppy seeds, she warns, or they will be too hard. Her husband requests this cake for special occasions, and once, for her father's birthday, she made two frostings, one sour cream and one chocolate, frosting the cake in two halves so everyone could pick their favorite side!

FOR THE CAKE

4 large eggs

1 cup (165 g) poppy seeds

1 cup (125 g) all-purpose flour

1 teaspoon baking soda

1 cup (200 g) sugar

1 cup (240 ml) kefir or buttermilk

3 tablespoons cognac

FOR THE FROSTING
(MAKES 4 CUPS/960 ML)

4 cups (960 ml) full-fat sour cream

½ cup (100 g) sugar

2 tablespoons cognac

1 tablespoon vanilla extract

2 tablespoons poppy seeds

1. *Make the cake.* Whisk the eggs and the poppy seeds in the bowl of a standing mixer until the eggs are light and the poppy seeds are fully incorporated, about 4 minutes. Cover and refrigerate overnight.

2. Preheat the oven to 350°F (175°C). Thoroughly grease three 8-inch (20-cm) round pans.

3. Whisk the flour and baking soda in a medium bowl and set aside.

4. Remove the egg mixture from the refrigerator and whisk to re-combine. Whisk in the sugar, then the kefir. Whisk the flour mixture into the egg mixture.

5. Divide the batter evenly among the three pans. Bake for 15 minutes, until the edges begin to brown. Remove and cool completely in the pans on a wire rack.

6. Once cool, remove the cakes from the pans and trim any brown edges. Using a cake tester, poke holes all over the cakes. Brush 1 tablespoon cognac on each layer.

7. *Make the frosting.* Using a stand or hand mixer with the whisk attachment, whisk together the sour cream, sugar, cognac, and vanilla until very firm.

8. To assemble, place one cake layer on a serving dish and cover with one quarter of the frosting (about 1 cup/240 ml) and spread. Place a second cake layer on top and spread with another quarter of the frosting. Place the final cake layer on top. Cover with a generous helping of frosting, and use it to cover the top and sides—you may not need all of the frosting. Sprinkle the poppy seeds all over.

9. Chill for at least two hours, or up to overnight, before serving.

Marina's Stuffed Cabbage

serves — 8 TO 10 (MAKES ABOUT 24 CABBAGE ROLLS) | *PREP* 30 MINUTES | *TOTAL* 1 HOUR AND 40 MINUTES

FILLED WITH LAMB, beef, and rice and smothered in a deeply flavored tomato cream sauce, this cabbage dish is worth the effort. Marina cooks a large batch, then saves the leftover cabbage leaves to make "Lazy Man's" stuffed cabbage another day: Instead of stuffing the cabbage, she sautés it with the meat and covers it with sauce for a quicker and easier alternative!

2 medium green cabbages (2 pounds/ 907 g each)

2 tablespoons extra-virgin olive oil

3 large carrots, grated on the large holes of a box grater (about 2 cups/220 g)

1 large onion, finely minced (about 2 cups/220 g)

1 pound (455 g) ground lamb

1 pound (455 g) ground 90% lean beef

¾ cup (145 g) medium-grain rice, cooked to yield 1½ cup (195 g) rice

Coarse salt

Freshly ground black pepper

2 tablespoons chopped dill

2 tablespoons chopped cilantro

4 cups (960 ml) tomato sauce

2 cups (480 ml) sour cream

1. Bring 8 cups (2 L) water to a boil in a large pot. Prepare an ice bath in a large bowl.

2. Pierce the base of the cabbage with a large fork and use it to lower the cabbage into the boiling water for three minutes. Remove from the water and plunge it into the ice bath; keep the water at a boil. Lift it out and begin removing the cabbage leaves, setting them on a plate to dry. Once you reach layers that resist easy removal, lower the remaining cabbage into the boiling water for 3 more minutes. Remove, plunge it into the ice bath, and peel off the rest of the leaves. Repeat with the second cabbage.

3. Shave down the rib of each leaf to make it more pliable. Only the larger leaves should be used for stuffing—the very small, inner core leaves can be saved for another use (like Marina's Lazy Man version!).

4. Preheat the oven to 350°F (175°C).

5. While the leaves dry, heat the olive oil in a large sauté pan over medium heat. Add the carrots and onion and cook until the onion is translucent and the carrot begins to brown slightly, about 8 minutes. Remove from the heat and let cool. Divide the mixture in half.

6. Combine both meats with the rice in a large bowl. Add half of the carrot mixture with 1 teaspoon salt, 1 teaspoon pepper, the dill, and the cilantro. Mix thoroughly.

7. Take a large cabbage leaf and lay it rib side down. Pile 2 heaping tablespoons of filling at one side. Fold in the two sides and roll up the leaf. Repeat until all the mixture has been used.

8. Set the stuffed cabbages in rows in two 9 × 13-inch (23 × 33-cm) baking dishes.

9. Whisk together the reserved carrot mixture, tomato sauce, sour cream, 1 tablespoon salt, and 1 tablespoon pepper. Pour over the stuffed cabbage.

10. Bake uncovered for 40 minutes and serve with the sauce that has collected in the dish over the top.

MARINA VARSHISKY

ANKE GELBIN

◆

WHEN ANKE JACOBS GELBIN LEFT the hustle and bustle of downtown Berlin to come to the United States, she thought it would be a quick, one-year adventure. However, American life agreed with her family, and one year turned into twenty-seven and counting.

Anke's husband, Michael, has American roots, so while they were still living in Berlin, they felt it was important that their two children, Laura and Ruben, have a firm grasp of English. When the opportunity arose to come to the States, this proved beneficial, as the transition wasn't quite as challenging. Anke recounted how her son met some children shortly after they arrived and came back to their apartment to exclaim, "Mom, they all speak English here!"

Because they already had a firm footing in their new language, Anke realized that it was German that she would need to reinforce at home. (She even made a little sign that read, "We only speak German at this table" for their nightly meals.) Keeping their German culture at the forefront was important to her. Every night, she would cook the food of her homeland so that along with German speaking, there was lots of German eating. Her goulash (page 55) is still a family favorite, and she makes it as a special treat whenever she visits her son and daughter.

Anke's Goulash
(BEEF STEW)

serves 6 TO 8 | PREP 15 MINUTES | TOTAL 1 HOUR AND 30 MINUTES

AS A BUSY, working mother, Anke adapted her goulash recipe for a pressure cooker so she could come home from a busy day at work and still have dinner on the table in less than an hour. For those of us who haven't mastered the pressure cooker, I adapted the recipe for a Dutch oven. It's a true one-pot wonder—serve it with some buttered German spaetzle or boiled potatoes sprinkled with salt.

3½ pounds (1.6 kg) beef round (stew meat), cut into 2-inch (5-cm) pieces

2 tablespoons coarse salt

2 teaspoons freshly ground black pepper

3 tablespoons vegetable oil

1 medium white onion, diced

1 cup (240 ml) sour cream

2 garlic cloves, minced

1 tablespoon Hungarian paprika

1 tablespoon tomato paste

Pinch of cayenne, or more to taste

1 teaspoon chopped parsley, for garnish

1. Season the meat with the salt and pepper. Heat 2 tablespoons of the vegetable oil in a Dutch oven or pressure cooker over medium-high heat and, in batches, brown the meat on all sides, about 4 minutes per batch.

2. Add the onion to the pot and cook, stirring, until slightly browned, then add the sour cream. Stir until the meat is covered in a brown sauce (gravy).

3. Add the garlic, paprika, tomato paste, and cayenne.

4. Pour water to cover the meat by 1 to 2 inches (2.5 to 5 cm). Bring to a boil, then reduce the heat and simmer until the meat is very tender. In a Dutch oven, this will take about 1 hour. In a pressure cooker, it will take 15 minutes on high pressure.

5. Remove the lid and turn the heat to high. Boil for another 15 minutes, stirring occasionally, to thicken the cooking liquid.

6. Serve with buttered noodles (Anke likes Bechtle Bavarian-Style Spaetzle) or boiled potatoes and sprinkle with chopped parsley.

Anke brought this metric measuring cup with her to her new homeland to ensure she could continue making her family recipes without error.

ANKE GELBIN

Anke's German Potato Salad

serves 6 TO 8 | **PREP** 15 MINUTES | **TOTAL** 45 MINUTES

IF YOU GOOGLE "German Potato Salad," countless versions show up in the nearly one million results. According to Anke, each German home has its own version—even her grandmother's was a bit different—and I was intrigued by Anke's take, a throwback to her mother's version.

Anke has a meticulous approach to composing her salad. As a respected chemist, she brings science into the kitchen, so you know the formula will work. But even the best science involves experimentation, so this recipe allows you to add a little more mayo here, a little more mustard there, then more mayo, and finally a pinch of salt or a grind of pepper, until the flavor is just right. Anke suggests making this dish the day before so the flavors have time to meld. It's perfect for entertaining and is a wonderful side dish to German sausages.

2 to 3 pounds (907 g to 1.4 kg) Yukon Gold potatoes

1 small red onion, minced

6 to 7 small Polish dill pickles, diced

6 to 7 tablespoons (90 to 105 ml) mayonnaise

4 teaspoons Dijon mustard

Coarse salt

Freshly ground black pepper

1. Fill a medium pot with water, boil, and cook potatoes for 8 to 10 minutes, until fork-tender.

2. Allow potatoes to cool enough to handle, about 5 minutes, then peel and cut them into small cubes.

3. Combine the potatoes, red onion, and pickles in a large bowl. Carefully fold in the mayonnaise and mustard. The potatoes should not be overly dressed, but you do want to taste the mayonnaise and mustard. Season with salt and pepper gradually to your liking.

4. Serve cold or at room temperature.

Note

Make sure to get good dill pickles and use Hellman's mayonnaise—it makes all the difference!

ANKE GELBIN

56

EUROPE | *Berlin, Germany*

SUSANNE KIDD

◆

SUSANNE IS A GERMAN IMMIGRANT who came to the United States in her early twenties. She married, raised two children, and like all of the women I have cooked with, embraced the American dream. While her children, Christina and Jonathan, were young, Susanne went to law school at night and graduated at the top of her class. Not only is she a successful attorney, but she recently completed a rigorous program at New York University in language translation to prepare herself for a second career once she retires.

Although she is tirelessly active and engaged with her work, her most important wish for retirement is to spend more time with her beautiful grandchildren. In her free time, she knits, weaves, and of course teaches the little ones about their German heritage and culture. Frequent trips with her family to Hamburg to visit her mother give Susanne's grandchildren a sense of where they come from through continued education in the German language, culture, and, of course, good food.

Susanne's Schmorgurken
(GROUND MEAT WITH BRAISED CUCUMBERS)

serves 6 | *PREP* 10 MINUTES | *TOTAL* 40 MINUTES

THIS HEARTY STEW, called *schmorgurken*, is a favorite in Germany. According to Susanne, Germans love to squish the potatoes up as they eat to sop up the savory, meaty broth. The glassy cucumbers provide an interesting and delicious element.

4 cucumbers (not English/hothouse)

1 tablespoon vegetable oil

1 pound (455 g) ground 90% lean beef, pork, veal, or a mix

Coarse salt

Freshly ground black pepper

1 garlic clove, minced

1 (28-ounce/794-g) can whole peeled tomatoes, drained and chopped (or 6 Roma tomatoes, peeled)

1 (14.5-ounce/410-g) can unsalted chicken, beef, or vegetable broth

2 tablespoons apple cider vinegar

2 tablespoons sugar

¼ cup (13 g) finely chopped fresh dill

2 large potatoes (about 1 pound/455 g), peeled, quartered, and boiled

Crème fraîche or sour cream

1. Peel and halve the cucumbers lengthwise. Then, seed and cut them into small, bite-size pieces. Set aside.

2. Heat the oil in a large pot over medium heat and cook the ground meat until browned, breaking it up with a wooden spoon. Season with ½ teaspoon each salt and pepper.

3. Add the garlic and the cucumbers and cook until they start to look a bit translucent, about 5 minutes.

4. Add the tomatoes and cook for 2 to 3 minutes. Add the broth and bring to a simmer. Cook for about 15 minutes, until the cucumbers are soft but not mushy.

5. Stir in the vinegar and sugar, and season to taste with additional salt and pepper. Add the dill.

6. Serve with boiled potatoes and a dollop of crème fraîche or sour cream on top.

Susanne's Rollfleisch

(ROLLED FILLED BEEF)

serves 6 | **PREP** 15 MINUTES | *TOTAL* 1½ HOURS

THIS DISH WAS a favorite in Susanne's family when she was growing up. When it came time to eat, she remembers her father's exasperation over pulling the twine off the roll—inevitably, every time the beef rolled over, his Sunday shirt would get splattered with gravy. Once, her mother had double-rolled the beef, and in protest, her father stood on his chair as he unraveled it. So, take a bit of advice from Susanne's beloved father, and stand back when it's time to eat!

¾ pound (340 g) green beans

12 (¼-inch/6-mm thick) slices top round or bottom round beef or any lean meat, pounded to 10 x 6 x ⅛ inches (25 x 15 x .3 cm)

Coarse salt

Freshly ground black pepper

6 teaspoons spicy brown mustard (Suzanne likes Gulden's)

12 slices bacon, center cut

12 cornichons, or 3 large pickles quartered lengthwise

2 carrots, peeled and cut into thin 3-inch (7.5-cm) sticks

1 small onion, cut in half and sliced into 3-inch (7.5-cm) pieces

2 tablespoons vegetable oil

1 tablespoon unsalted butter

1 tablespoon lemon juice

¼ cup (13 g) chopped parsley

2 to 3 tablespoons sour cream

Buttered egg noodles or boiled small potatoes

1. **Prepare the green beans.** Trim the ends and cook them in shallow boiling water for 3 to 4 minutes. Drain and set aside.

2. Lightly sprinkle each slice of beef with salt and pepper, and spread each with ½ teaspoon of the mustard.

3. Place a slice of bacon on each slice of meat, lengthwise, trimming it so it doesn't stick out. Save the trimmings.

4. Across the middle of each slice, place a small pickle, 2 to 3 carrot sticks, and 1 to 2 pieces of onion. Save any leftover onion.

5. Roll up the meat and secure with twine or toothpicks at each end to make sure none of the filling falls out during cooking. Store in the refrigerator until ready to cook if not making immediately.

6. When ready to cook, heat the oil in a large sauté pan over medium heat. Brown the meat rolls on all sides, about 5 minutes. Add any leftover bacon and onion and sauté for another 3 minutes.

7. Pour 1 cup (240 ml) water over the rolls and scrape up any bits stuck to the bottom of the pan. Bring to a boil, then reduce to a gentle simmer. Cook for 1 hour, covered, checking the liquid level every 15 minutes. Add more water as necessary so the rolls are in enough liquid to make a gravy.

8. When 15 minutes remain, melt the butter in a medium pot over medium heat and add the green beans. Salt and pepper to taste. Add the lemon juice and parsley and stir to coat.

9. When the beef is done, remove the rolls from the pan and place on a serving dish. Add the sour cream to the pan sauce and season with salt and pepper.

10. Remove the toothpicks from the rolled beef and pour the sauce over the rolls. Serve with the string beans and buttered egg noodles.

Susanne's Appelkoken

(APPLE DONUTS)

makes 40 | **PREP** 1 HOUR AND 10 MINUTES | **TOTAL** 1 HOUR AND 20 MINUTES

SUSANNE REMEMBERS HELPING her beloved grandmother, Oma Hildegard, make these delicious little apple donuts every New Year's Eve. When it was time to cook, they gathered the essential tools: a large ceramic bowl for mixing, a warm radiator for rising, the big wooden spoon for mixing, and some knitting needles for flipping. These were the critical components to get the recipe just right.

Susanne's job was to fetch the apples, leftover from the fall harvest, from the cellar. The apples may have been a bit wrinkled, but with a good peeling and a fine chop, they were ready to drop into the batter with the rum raisins and fine vanilla sugar. As the baker's helper, she had the important task of tasting the first batch to make sure they were perfectly cooked. Then they were showered with powdered sugar and served to the lucky New Year's guests while still warm.

In order to make these special treats, an aebleskiver pan is needed. I purchased mine, as well as a pair of turning tools (I don't knit! Chopsticks are another good alternative), and got to work. The result? Perfect little spheres that melt in your mouth and cover your lips with white powder. I got better as I went, each round of donuts looking better than the last. By the end, they were rounder, lighter, and even more delicious than the first. I couldn't eat just one!

½ cup (75 g) raisins

2 tablespoons white rum

3 cups (375 g) all-purpose flour

1 envelope (2½ teaspoons/ 7 g) active dry yeast

½ cup plus 1 tablespoon (106 g) sugar (see Note)

1½ cups plus 2 tablespoons (390 ml) warm whole milk

7 tablespoons (99 g) unsalted butter, softened

2 large eggs

1 teaspoon vanilla bean paste or vanilla extract

⅛ teaspoon salt

Zest and juice of 1 lemon

2 tart apples, peeled and chopped into ¼-inch (6-mm) dice (Susanne prefers Granny Smith)

Vegetable shortening

Confectioners' sugar

Note

Instead of using the sugar and vanilla bean paste, vanilla sugar can be made in advance by simply leaving a vanilla bean in the sugar overnight. If you use this sugar, omit the vanilla bean paste.

Continues

1. Combine the raisins and rum in a small bowl. Let sit until the raisins become plump.

2. Place the flour in a large bowl and make a well in the center. Place the yeast, 1 tablespoon of the sugar, and 2 tablespoons of the milk into the well. Carefully whisk the yeast mixture in the well until the yeast dissolves. Place in a warm place, covered with a kitchen towel, for 10 minutes. The mixture should bubble slightly.

3. Gradually mix the flour into the well with a wooden spoon until the mixture is fully incorporated.

4. Add the remaining milk and sugar plus the butter, eggs, vanilla, salt, lemon zest, and lemon juice, and mix thoroughly with a wooden spoon until the batter is bubbly and drips slowly from the spoon. If the batter is too thick, add a bit more warm milk until it reaches the correct consistency (a very thick pancake batter, as at right).

5. Drain the raisins and mix them into the batter along with the apples. Cover the bowl with a kitchen towel and let the batter rise in a warm place until it doubles in size, 40 to 50 minutes.

6. Heat the aebleskiver pan over medium heat, add a pea-sized amount of shortening to each well, and wait for it to sizzle a bit. Ladle batter into each well, enough to just reach the rim. The shortening will bubble around the sides and the appelkoken will begin to brown. A wooden stick, like a chopstick, is useful in tilting it slightly to check on color, which should be light brown.

7. While the center is still soft, use the wooden stick to turn the appelkoken over. Cook for 2 more minutes, then check for doneness by inserting a toothpick in the middle. It should come out clean.

8. Remove the donuts from the pan and place them in a flat bowl or on a plate, and dust with confectioners' sugar, turning each appelkoken to cover. Repeat with the remaining batter.

Note

As an appelkoken novice, I found I had to play with the amount of heat to ensure the inside of the donut was cooked before the outside became too dark. If you find this happening, you can preheat the oven to 350°F (177°C) and finish them off in the oven for 5 minutes once the outsides are golden brown—I promise not to tell Oma!

SUSANNE KIDD

KANELLA "NELLY" CHELIOTIS

When you walk into a Greek American home, you immediately feel the love and dedication the family maintains for Greece.

PICTURES AND MEMENTOS OF TRIPS to the homeland decorate the walls, as many Greeks make annual trips to visit family and friends. This pride starts at home at an early age and spreads through extended family and the broader community, typically with a local Greek Orthodox church at its center. In order to preserve their heritage, many Greek Americans send their children to the local church's "Greek school" two to three times per week. This formal education includes learning the language, traditions, religion, and history of Greece. The result is that many Greek Americans in first- and second-generation homes are immersed in the culture and traditions of their ancestors and adopt a lifelong pride in the Hellenic way of life.

I believe this deep pride in Greek culture is the reason my dear friend Kostas was the first to sign his mother, Kanella, up for this project. Nelly, as she is known, was born on the southern Greek peninsula of Peloponnese. She grew up in a very small town located on a mountain overlooking the Mediterranean called Pigadi, a village with only twenty families. The town did not have electricity until after she left for America in the seventies. She began cooking alongside her mother at the age of six, because, as Nelly explained, "there was nothing else to do in my village!" She married at nineteen, and the young bride left her childhood home and headed out to follow the promise of a better life in the United States with her husband, Athanasios (Tommy).

She began her new life in Park Slope, Brooklyn, in 1971. She and her husband rented a small apartment for $60 per month. Nelly quickly sought work as a seamstress, and obtained a position at the Petrocelli suit factory. She continued working there full time as her family grew and eventually moved to Long Island. She would take the bus into Manhattan five days a week, work, come home, and cook for her family every night. After years of working and saving every nickel, in 1981 Nelly and her husband bought a local diner in Valley Stream, New York, which they operated with other family members as cooks, waiters, and employees. But Nelly explained that she never cooked for the diner. Only those that she loves and cares for—her children, Diane and Kostas, in-laws, grandchildren, and those who attend her church festivals—get to eat her food.

I asked her about the cuisine of her home and she said, "I only cook Greek food, my food. My children and grandchildren eat my food every day." Nelly graciously and enthusiastically taught me how to make several Greek staples, including two kinds of spanakopita (spinach-and-cheese pastry): the spanakopita we are familiar with in the United States (page 66) and real Greek spanakopita. The traditional Greek spanakopita is always made at home for family dinners. It is made with homemade phyllo dough and no butter, which is not a staple ingredient in a Greek home—olive oil is used for all cooking. Olive oil is so essential to a successful Greek recipe that Nelly's entrepreneurial daughter-in-law Katina now bottles it and sells it in the United States under the name Kosterina!

After we finished cooking, Nelly declared, "Okay, now we eat!" It felt like a holiday! Sitting down to dinner with her happy, loving family was just like sitting at my mother's table—that same feeling of "the more the merrier," everyone eats together, and of course, nothing is more important than eating the foods you cherish with the people you love.

NELLY'S "CHURCH FESTIVAL"
Spanakopita

serves 8 TO 10 | *PREP* 30 MINUTES | *TOTAL* 1 HOUR AND 30 MINUTES

WHEN YOU THINK of Greek food, spanakopita immediately comes to mind. However, for Greeks, spanakopita is not those small little triangle canapés you find at weddings and cocktail parties. Instead, it's a larger dish eaten regularly with family and friends. Nelly loves eating it in the afternoon with a nice glass of wine.

Through adaptation and migration, the recipe has been altered from its traditional preparation. While Greek Americans still make it in a large pan, they swapped frozen spinach for fresh, began buying boxed phyllo instead of making it themselves, and brushed the layers with butter instead of olive oil. The substitutions yield buttery, crispy phyllo sheets that perfectly counterbalance a creamy, salty spinach filling.

FOR THE FILLING

4 tablespoons (½ stick/ 55 g) butter

5 scallions, chopped

4 pounds (1.8 kg) frozen chopped spinach, defrosted

½ bunch dill, chopped (about 1 cup/50 g)

1 teaspoon salt

1 teaspoon freshly ground black pepper

5 large eggs, beaten

1 pound (455 g) cottage cheese

1½ pounds (680 g) feta cheese, broken up into small pieces

½ cup (120 ml) extra-virgin olive oil

FOR THE DOUGH

1 to 1¼ cups (240 to 300 ml) clarified butter

1 package phyllo dough, #4 (Nelly likes Apollo)

1. Preheat the oven to 375°F (190°C).

2. **Prepare the filling.** Melt the butter in a small pan over medium heat, then cook the scallions until soft and translucent, 3 to 5 minutes. Transfer to a large bowl and let cool.

3. Thoroughly drain the spinach of all water by squeezing it in a cheesecloth. (Wet spinach will cause your spanakopita to be soggy.)

4. Add the spinach, dill, salt, pepper, eggs, cottage cheese, feta cheese, and olive oil to the bowl containing the scallions. Fold the ingredients together until fully combined, being careful not to break up the feta. Set aside.

5. **Prepare the dough.** Using the melted, clarified butter, lightly butter a 10 × 15-inch (25 × 38-cm) baking dish or baking sheet. Remove the phyllo from the package, unfurl each piece, and lay flat. You should have around 25 to 30 sheets. As you work, cover the flattened dough sheets with a damp tea towel or moistened paper towel to prevent them from drying out.

6. Carefully peel off one sheet of phyllo and lay it on the bottom of the dish. Do not straighten or pull tight. With a pastry brush, generously spread clarified butter over the sheet until it is moistened. Continue laying down sheets and coating with butter until you have used half of your total phyllo dough (10 to 15 sheets).

Continues

KANELLA CHELIOTIS

Spread the spinach filling over the phyllo in an even layer.

Brush clarified butter on the top layer, into each cut, and around the borders.

Sharp cuts ensure perfect triangular bites.

Flaky, buttery phyllo sheets perfectly balance the creamy spinach filling.

NELLY'S SECRETS FOR THE
PERFECT SPANAKOPITA

Clarify the butter ◆ *"It is an extra step, but it is very important. It creates a beautiful shiny finish to the top layer. Otherwise, the butter will brown unevenly."*

Make sure the spinach is dry ◆ *The most important step is ensuring the spinach is completely defrosted and very dry. Use cheesecloth to drain it so that you don't end up with a watery filling and a soggy final product.*

Fix soggy filling ◆ *If your filling still looks watery after you finish mixing, add a tablespoon of uncooked rice. It will absorb the liquid during cooking and you will never taste it!*

Get creative ◆ *Throw a bunch of chicory or escarole into the mix. Chicory was her husband Tommy's favorite—he liked the way the bitterness of the chicory counterbalanced the mild spinach.*

7. Spread the spinach filling over the sheets of phyllo in an even layer, to the edges of the dish.

8. Layer the remaining phyllo sheets, brushing with butter between each layer, until 3 sheets of phyllo remain. Place the final sheets on top together, tightly, to create a smooth top. Brush the top with clarified butter to finish.

9. Using a very sharp paring knife, score four even lines lengthwise down the phyllo about ½ inch (12 mm) deep. Then cut five even lines across horizontally, to create 30 rectangular pieces. Cut a diagonal line across each piece to create triangles. Nelly likes to cut the corner pieces in opposite directions, as in the photo at left.

10. Brush clarified butter into each cut. This keeps the phyllo in place while cooking. Using the paring knife, carefully tuck the borders down by running the knife around all four edges. Brush the borders with butter.

11. Bake for 1 hour, until the top is a deep golden brown. (Check after 45 minutes to assess the level of browning. If it is already dark brown, cover with foil for the last 15 minutes of cooking.) Let cool; serve at room temperature.

◆

KANELLA CHELIOTIS

Nelly's Pastitsio

serves — 8 | PREP 40 MINUTES | TOTAL 1 HOUR AND 25 MINUTES

PASTITSIO IS A very popular baked pasta dish that is said to have origins in Venice, Italy. After tasting it, I immediately thought that this dish tastes as if lasagna Bolognese and fettuccini Alfredo had a delicious love child.

FOR THE MEAT SAUCE

2 tablespoons Greek olive oil (Nelly prefers Kosterina)

1½ pounds (680 g) ground beef (93 percent lean)

1 small onion, finely diced

1 (8-ounce/240 ml) can tomato sauce

1 tablespoon coarse salt

Freshly ground black pepper

½ stick cinnamon

5 to 6 whole allspice berries

FOR THE BÉCHAMEL

½ cup (1 stick/115 g) unsalted butter

¼ cup (30 g) all-purpose flour

5 cups (1.2 L) milk, heated until just simmering

2 teaspoons coarse salt

½ teaspoon nutmeg

4 large eggs, beaten

2 tablespoons pecorino Romano cheese

FOR THE PASTA

1 pound (455 g) ziti, cooked according to package directions, still warm

Extra-virgin olive oil

1 teaspoon coarse salt

2 tablespoons unsalted butter

2 large eggs, beaten

1 cup (240 ml) whole milk

Freshly ground black pepper

FOR ASSEMBLY

2 tablespoons unsalted butter, softened

3 tablespoons all-purpose flour

¼ cup plus 2 tablespoons (37 g) grated pecorino Romano cheese

2 teaspoons ground nutmeg

1. **Make the meat sauce.** Heat 1 tablespoon of the olive oil in large sauté pan over medium heat. Add the ground beef and cook until no pink remains. Remove from the pan and drain the meat.

2. Add the remaining tablespoon olive oil to the pan and cook the onion over medium heat until translucent, 5 to 7 minutes, then return the meat to the pan.

3. Add the tomato sauce, salt, pepper, cinnamon stick, and allspice. Cook until the ingredients are incorporated, about 15 minutes. Nelly adds ¼ cup (60 ml) water if the meat begins to dry out. Divide the mixture in half.

4. **While the meat is cooking, make the béchamel.** Melt the butter in a large saucepan over medium heat until it begins to bubble. Add the flour and whisk until it turns light brown. Slowly add the milk one cup at a time, whisking constantly. Add the salt and nutmeg, stir, and remove from the heat.

5. Slowly add the beaten eggs while continuing to whisk. Once the eggs are incorporated, place the mixture back over medium heat and bring it to a boil. Add the pecorino and mix until incorporated. Remove from the heat.

6. *Prepare the pasta.* Place the cooked ziti in a large bowl and coat with a drizzle of olive oil and the salt.

7. Add the butter and mix until melted. Then add the eggs, half of the beef mixture, milk, and pepper. Set aside.

8. *Assemble the pastitsio.* Preheat the oven to 400°F (205°C).

9. Butter a 10 × 15-inch (25 × 38-cm) baking dish and then sprinkle it with flour. Pour the pasta into the bottom of the dish in an even layer. Spread the remaining meat sauce evenly over the pasta. Sprinkle the ¼ cup of pecorino over the meat.

10. Carefully pour the béchamel over the meat and spread it with an offset spatula. Sprinkle with the nutmeg and the remaining pecorino.

11. Bake uncovered for 40 to 45 minutes, until golden and bubbly.

Every home in Kanella's village had a coffee grinder. This one belonged to her grandmother, Kanella Chiotis, and is now one of her most cherished mementos.

Kanella and Athanasios surrounded by Kanella's family on their wedding day, 1971.

KANELLA CHELIOTIS

71

Nelly's Makaronia me Kima

(SPAGHETTI WITH MEAT SAUCE)

serves 6 | PREP 15 MINUTES | TOTAL 45 MINUTES

ONCE WE FINISHED the meat sauce for Pastitsio (page 70), Nelly set aside a cupful. I immediately questioned why. "I am saving this for [my son] Kostas. I will put it over some pasta for lunch." "Oh," I replied, "like pasta Bolognese?" "No," she laughed, "for *makaronia me kima*." So, here is the recipe for what *I* call Greek Pasta Bolognese!

2 tablespoons Greek olive oil (Nelly prefers Kosterina)

1½ pounds (680 g) ground beef (93 percent lean)

1 small onion, finely diced

1 (8-ounce/240-ml) can tomato sauce

1 tablespoon coarse salt

Freshly ground black pepper

½ stick cinnamon

5 to 6 whole allspice berries

1 pound (455 g) thin spaghetti

¼ cup (25 g) grated pecorino Romano or kefalotyri cheese

1. Heat 1 tablespoon of the olive oil in a large sauté pan over medium heat. Add the ground beef and cook until no pink remains. Remove from the pan and drain the meat.

2. Add the remaining tablespoon olive oil to the pan and cook the onion over medium heat until translucent, 5 to 7 minutes, then return the meat to the pan.

3. Add the tomato sauce, salt, pepper, cinnamon stick, and allspice. Cook until the ingredients are incorporated, about 15 minutes. Nelly adds ¼ cup (60 ml) water if the meat begins to dry out.

4. Bring 8 cups (2 L) water to a boil in a large pot and cook the spaghetti according to the package instructions. Drain the pasta, reserving ½ cup (120 ml) of the pasta water.

5. Combine the pasta and meat sauce with the pasta water in the pot.

6. Serve with grated cheese.

MONIKA SZYDLOWSKI

◆

MONIKA SZYDLOWSKI CAME TO THE United States after college to continue her education. Although she loved her home in Poland, she strove for something new and exciting. She met her husband, Grzegorz, also a Polish immigrant, in the United States, and together they worked hard to establish roots in their new shared home, traveling back to Poland often to visit family. She worked diligently to learn English, raise her daughter, Natalia, and create a thriving photography business.

When discussing her homeland, Monika emphasizes how pure and clean the food of her childhood was. She grew up in the mountains on a big farm tended by her parents and grandparents. Everything they ate came from their soil. In Poland, potatoes and onions are staple crops, so it made sense that pierogies—potato and onion dumplings—were eaten weekly. ("You can grow a potato anywhere!" Monika joked.) She grew up making authentic Polish meals alongside her grandmother and mother. Every meal began with a hearty soup, usually vegetarian, followed by a meat course (from their own animals), a side of fresh vegetables from the garden, and some homemade sauerkraut.

Monika is proud of her Polish roots: She teaches Polish school on Sundays, cooks traditional food for the holidays, and even has a loyal following of other Polish transplants, as she's known for being able to type up Christmas cards in Polish to send back to family. Most importantly, she is also a true American woman, juggling career and family while also creating Polish and American food for dinner. Sometimes she likes to riff on her traditional pierogies (page 74) by adding spinach, Parmigiano cheese, or a dash of cayenne pepper (just don't tell her mother!).

MONIKA'S PERFECT
Pierogies

serves — 10 TO 12 (MAKES 50 PIEROGIES) | *PREP* 45 MINUTES | *TOTAL* 1 HOUR

I BELIEVE THE secret to Monika's perfect pierogies is the Polish flour. Unlike all-purpose flour, Polish flour is very fine and creates a melt-in-your-mouth dough. After trying them, I knew I had to know how to make them. So, I invited Monika to my home for a pierogi lesson. She came to my kitchen armed with ingredients from the Polish store in town and taught me how to make the most delicious pierogies I have ever tasted! Best of all, it's the same way her grandmother in Poland still makes them today. If she can't find Polish bacon, Monika uses pancetta in a pinch.

FOR THE DOUGH

3½ cups (420 g) Polish flour, or extra-fine flour with no additives, plus more for shaping

1 teaspoon extra-virgin olive oil

1 large egg, beaten

FOR THE FILLING AND TOPPING

6 medium Yukon Gold potatoes, peeled

¼ cup (60 ml) extra-virgin olive oil

4 ounces (115 g) Polish bacon or pancetta, finely diced

1 large yellow onion, finely diced

1 cup (8 ounces/227 g) farmer's cheese

Coarse salt

Freshly ground black pepper

Sour cream (optional)

1. *Make the dough.* Combine the flour and oil with 1½ cups (360 ml) boiling water in the bowl of an electric mixer with the paddle attachment. Add the egg and mix until combined.

2. Turn out the dough onto a floured surface and knead until the dough is soft and bounces back when pressed, about 10 minutes.

3. Place in a clean bowl and cover with a tea towel. Rest the dough for 10 minutes.

4. *Prepare the filling.* Add 10 cups of water to a large pot, salt it, and add the potatoes. Bring to a boil and cook until fork-tender, about 8 to 10 minutes.

5. Meanwhile, heat 1 tablespoon of the olive oil in a large saucepan over medium heat and add the bacon. Once the bacon begins to render, about 2 minutes, add the onion and cook over low heat until the onion is soft and beginning to brown, 10 more minutes.

6. Remove about half of the bacon mixture and mix it with the farmer's cheese in a large bowl. Set aside the remaining bacon mixture.

7. Add the potatoes to the bowl with the bacon mixture and farmer's cheese. Mash and mix until fully incorporated. Season with salt and pepper.

8. *Make the pierogies.* Cut the dough into 4 pieces and return 3 to the covered bowl. Roll out the first piece to about ⅛ inch (3 mm) thick. Using a water glass or a 2-inch (5-cm) cookie cutter, cut out circles from the dough, rerolling the scraps to use all of the dough. You will have about 12 circles.

9. Place about 1 tablespoon of filling into the middle of a dough circle. Cup the dough in your hand and fold the circle in half, enclosing the filling.

MONIKA SZYDLOWSKI

10. Place the half-moon on its side in the palm of your hand and pinch the ends of the dough to create a sealed border.

11. Repeat with the remaining dough and filling to make about 50 pierogies.

12. Bring a large pot of salted water to a boil. Drop 12 to 15 pierogies in the water. After the pierogies float, cook for 2 to 3 more minutes.

13. Remove from the water with a slotted spoon and place on a clean plate. Repeat with the remaining pierogies.

14. Heat 2 tablespoons of olive oil in a large sauté pan over medium heat. Add as many pierogies to the pan as will fit with the remaining bacon mixture and cook for a few minutes, so that it all heats through together in the pan. Repeat with the remaining pierogies, adding more oil as needed, or freeze extras in large plastic storage bags; they will keep up to 30 days.

15. Serve with sour cream, if desired.

MONIKA SZYDLOWSKI

75

Monika's Piernik Staropolski

(CHOCOLATE-ENROBED SPICE CAKE WITH PLUM BUTTER FILLING)

Serves 6 TO 8 | **PREP** 25 MINUTES | **TOTAL** 1 HOUR, PLUS 4 WEEKS AND 4 DAYS

THIS CAKE REALLY blew my mind. The batter sits for four weeks. (Yes, that's right, you mix up the batter and forget about it for *four weeks*.) Made all over Poland for the holidays, Polish mothers would mix it up in November—Monika does hers Thanksgiving weekend—to have it ready to bake for Christmas. After cutting and filling the cake with plum butter, it sits for another three to four days. It's truly a practice of patience, but most definitely worth the wait!

FOR THE SPICE BLEND
5 teaspoons cinnamon

2 teaspoons ginger

1½ teaspoons cloves

1½ teaspoons cardamom

1 teaspoon nutmeg

1 teaspoon allspice

½ teaspoon anise

FOR THE CAKE
1½ cups (12 ounces/360 ml) high-quality honey

¾ cup (150 g) granulated sugar

10 tablespoons (145 g) unsalted butter

3¾ cups (450 g) pastry flour

⅓ cup (80 ml) whole milk

1½ teaspoons baking soda

1 teaspoon coarse salt

2 large eggs, beaten

½ cup (75 g) raisins (optional)

1 cup (240 ml) store-bought plum butter

FOR THE TOPPING
1 cup (240 ml) heavy cream

1 cup (170 g) chopped milk chocolate

1 cup (120 g) toasted chopped walnuts (optional)

1. **Make the spice blend.** Combine all the ingredients for the spice blend in a bowl.

2. **Make the cake.** Combine the honey, sugar, and butter in a medium saucepan over medium heat and cook until all the sugar has dissolved. Remove from the stove and cool completely.

3. While the mixture cools, combine 2 tablespoons of the spice blend (reserve the rest for another use) and the flour, milk, baking soda, and salt.

4. Add the cooled honey mixture along with the beaten eggs and raisins (if using). Mix to combine all ingredients. Cover with plastic wrap and refrigerate for 4 weeks.

5. Preheat the oven to 350°F (175°C).

Continues

Monika's mother handwrote
these recipes for her before
she left Poland.

6. Remove the batter from the fridge and mix again.

7. Pour the batter into a 9 × 13-inch (23 × 33-cm) pan and bake for 45 minutes. Remove from the oven and cool completely in the pan on a wire rack.

8. Remove the cake from the pan and cut it in half horizontally. Place the bottom half back into the pan and spread with the plum butter, careful to spread close to the edges.

9. Place the top half back on the cake and cover the top with plastic wrap. Place a 9 × 13-inch (23 × 33-cm) baking sheet on top of the cake and add a few heavy cans on top as weights. Refrigerate for 3 to 4 days.

10. Place a wire rack over a baking sheet or parchment paper. Remove the cake from the pan and place on the wire rack.

11. *Make the chocolate glaze.* Heat the cream to a simmer, then pour over the chocolate in a large bowl. Stir to melt and combine.

12. Pour the chocolate over the cake and sprinkle with toasted walnuts, if using. Place in the refrigerator for 15 minutes to allow the chocolate to harden before moving to a serving platter.

◆

MONIKA SZYDLOWSKI

78

STACEY TAYLOR

◆

WHEN YOU ASK STACEY TAYLOR why she left her native Scotland, her answer is quite simple: She wanted to discover the unknown. She grew up in a place where life was comfortable, predictable, and Scottish familial roots ran deep. So, when it came time to venture off after college, she had an urge for the unfamiliar.

Stacey and her then-boyfriend Michael headed out to Australia when career opportunities to relocate came their way. She remembers her first time away from home fondly, and she really enjoyed the multiculturalism she found with travel. But when it came time to marry, the couple wanted to return home, so they headed back to Edinburgh to start a family.

It wasn't long, though, before the urge to travel arose again, and when the chance to move to Malaysia came, they decided to jump into a new adventure with their two small children, Max and Ava. As Stacey explained, she wanted her children to open their eyes to the whole world and see that it "continued on past the end of their street."

The Taylors traveled all over Asia while living in Malaysia: They visited Thailand, Cambodia, Hong Kong, and Vietnam. These trips became opportunities to teach her children about different cultures, religions, and socioeconomic statuses. She feels her children developed a broad, progressive view of the world—an education they experienced firsthand.

Once they decided to settle in the United States due to another job opportunity, Stacey continued to plan trips around the country. She loves how the United States is like fifty countries in one—each state has its own history, foods, and even accents! The Taylors are checking off new states with each new vacation they plan, building memories and meeting interesting people along the way.

Stacey is fiercely proud of her Scottish heritage and speaks with an infectious laugh and a lovely brogue. Her family lovingly calls her "the people's friend" because no matter where they go, Stacey finds people to chat with. Her time in Malaysia developed her belief in karma, and she tries to give back whatever she receives. She loves making her tablet (page 81) for friends and neighbors. In my opinion, the fudge-like treat truly represents who Stacey is: Scottish and very sweet. We could all use a friend with an open mind and worldview like Stacey's.

Stacey's Tablet

makes 24 (2-INCH/5-CM) SQUARES | **PREP** 5 MINUTES | **TOTAL** 2 HOURS AND 45 MINUTES

TABLET IS A very well-known treat in Scotland. Similar to fudge but a bit grainier, it is a super-sweet, semi-soft homemade candy. Stacey makes it often for her children and friends.

4 tablespoons (½ stick/ 55 g) unsalted butter, plus more for the pan

2 pounds (907 g) confectioners' sugar

1 cup (240 ml) whole milk

1 (14-ounce/397-g) can sweetened condensed milk

1. Thoroughly butter a 9 × 13-inch (23 × 33-cm) baking dish or sheet pan. Set aside.

2. Melt the butter over low heat in a large pot. Add the sugar and milk and whisk until smooth. Turn up the heat to medium and cook until bubbling, 6 to 7 more minutes.

3. Add the sweetened condensed milk and cook for about 30 more minutes, whisking frequently to prevent the sugar from crystalizing. Once the mixture reaches 220° to 230°F (105° to 110°C)—it will coat the back of a spoon and be a medium brown color—remove it from the heat.

4. Place a hand mixer into the pot and whisk on high for 5 minutes. The mixture should thicken to the consistency of pudding.

5. Pour the mixture into the prepared pan and let harden, around 1 hour. It will have a fudge-like consistency. Once the tablet is hard, it can be cut into 2-inch (5-cm) squares.

This pendant of Saint Christopher, the patron saint of travel, was given to Stacey by her mother before she left Scotland.

STACEY TAYLOR

Stacey's Cullen Skink

serves 4 AS AN APPETIZER, 2 AS A MAIN DISH | *PREP* 10 MINUTES | *TOTAL* 45 MINUTES

WHILE IT MIGHT have a peculiar name, cullen skink is a staple stew for the Scottish. Similar to New England clam chowder, it is creamy and thick with delicious chunks of smoky haddock. Stacey's nontraditional addition is a cup of frozen peas at the end. It's one of her tricks to get her children to eat a vegetable once in a while!

8 ounces (227 g) smoked haddock

1½ cups (360 ml) whole milk

1 tablespoon unsalted butter

1 large white onion, minced

6 medium red potatoes (about 2 pounds/907 g), peeled and cut into 1-inch (2.5-cm) chunks

1½ cups (360 ml) chicken stock

1 cup (135 g) frozen peas

Coarse salt

Freshly ground black pepper

1. Combine the haddock and milk in a small pot. Bring to a simmer over medium heat to warm the milk and heat up the haddock, 5 to 6 minutes. Remove the haddock to a plate and set aside. Reserve the milk.

2. Melt the butter over medium heat in a large pot, and cook the onion until translucent, about 8 minutes. Add the potatoes and sauté for 2 to 3 more minutes to soften but not brown.

3. Add the reserved milk and the chicken stock. Bring to a simmer and cook for 20 minutes, until the potatoes are soft and the liquid has thickened.

4. Add the frozen peas and stir to combine and defrost, 3 to 4 minutes.

5. Flake the haddock from the skin and remove any pin bones. Add to the soup and stir, careful to not break up the haddock too much. Season with salt and pepper to taste. Serve immediately.

BEA PISKER TRIFUNAC

Today, it is easy to take the strides women have made in education and professional development for granted.

BUT IN OUR NOT-SO-DISTANT past, women were not encouraged to study and rise to the top of their class, and many remember a time when women were simply expected to raise children and keep the home tidy. Luckily, there were those who paved the way by rising to the challenge and who helped change the conversation for future generations.

Bea Trifunac is one of these women. Now retired, she completed her career as the director of an undergraduate lab at the California Institute of Technology in Pasadena. The last course she taught before retiring was Genetic Engineering.

What led Bea to this impressive career was a childhood devoted to study and scholastic excellence. Her father, Voja, always emphasized how important excelling in her studies would be for her future. He taught her that education fosters independence, and regardless of how talented or intelligent her future husband may be, having her own skills was of the utmost importance. In addition, Bea was never required to work as a child so long as she focused on her studies. Her parents' support and encouragement led her to be among the best in her class and to attend a highly regarded high school. After high school, she entered the University of Belgrade as a chemistry major. Her independent spirit, combined with her work ethic, led her to apply and be accepted into a graduate program at Caltech, where she was one of only thirty-five women accepted into the entire program.

While Bea was in California working on her degree, she missed her family in Serbia and craved her mother, Greta's, delicious food. Well-known by friends and family as an incredibly talented home cook, Greta worked as a language interpreter, but she was always in the kitchen making food for her husband and two daughters. When Bea visits her homeland today, family members and old friends will still mention her mother's incredible meals.

Soon, Bea began writing her mother for guidance in the kitchen, because after years of focused study, she found herself with the desire to cook but a lack of skills. During her mother's visits to America, she would give Bea instructions on preparing their family dishes and would also send her letters with recipes attached. Her childhood dishes recreated in her little American kitchen allowed her to infuse a semblance of home amid her rigorous studies. Foods of our childhood, "comfort foods," provide us with just that—comfort and a sense of stability when we need it most.

Bea's cooking repertoire is interesting because her varied ancestry has armed her with dishes from more than one country. Simply put, her familial roots are Austro-Hungarian, but at the age of two, Bea's family moved to Belgrade, Serbia, so her family's dishes were infused with Serbian, Austrian, and Hungarian flavors. Two of Bea's mother's specialties were paprikash (page 91), well-known in Hungary, and homemade burek (page 90), a popular layered phyllo dish from Serbia.

They also had their special desserts, and one of the dishes Bea's children, Irena and Sasha, have always cherished is Palacinka Torta (page 93), a "Swedish" crepe cake where egg whites are beaten into fluffy clouds and mixed with a bit of flour. Decadent yet light, Bea's daughter recounted how after the cake was made, she, her mother, and brother would each get up in the night to have an additional small slice. By morning, the cake would be gone and no one would seem to know how it had disappeared.

Bea has no idea why her mother called this cake "Swedish," because she found a similar recipe in her trusty Serbian cookbook, which is over forty years old. But like Bea's eclectic family origins, the cake has many layers!

BEA'S CHEESE AND DILL

Danish

---

serves 6 TO 8 AS AN APPETIZER (PER DANISH; MAKES 3 LARGE DANISHES) | *PREP* 1 HOUR | *TOTAL* 1 HOUR AND 45 MINUTES

AFTER MAKING THE dough for this savory dish, Bea expertly braids it over the filling. The final product is a glossy, beautiful Danish stuffed with a creamy cheese filling. This recipe makes three stunning Danish, so bake one and then freeze the other two for a future snack in less than an hour!

FOR THE DOUGH

1 teaspoon active dry yeast

½ teaspoon salt

½ teaspoon sugar

¾ cup (180 ml) warm milk

1½ cups plus 3 tablespoons (230 g) bread flour

1½ cups plus 3 tablespoons (213 g) all-purpose flour

14 tablespoons (1¾ sticks/196 g) unsalted butter, at room temperature

1 large egg

1 large egg yolk

FOR THE FILLING

2 (7.5-ounce/215-g) packages farmer's cheese

1 cup (240 ml) sour cream

2 large eggs

1 bunch dill, finely chopped, or 2 cups (100 g)

1 teaspoon salt

1 tablespoon all-purpose flour

FOR THE TOPPING

1 large egg, beaten (for egg wash)

1 tablespoon caraway seeds

1 tablespoon large-flake salt

1. Mix the yeast, salt, and sugar into the warm milk and let stand for 10 minutes.

2. Combine the flours and butter in the bowl of a standing mixer with a paddle attachment. Add the egg and egg yolk, then the milk mixture. Mix until a soft dough just forms. Roll the dough into a large ball with your hands, place it in a bowl, cover the bowl with plastic wrap, and refrigerate for 30 minutes.

3. *While the dough is resting, make the filling.* Combine all of the ingredients for the filling by hand in a large mixing bowl. Divide the mixture into 3 equal parts and set aside.

4. *Make the Danish.* Preheat the oven to 375°F (190°C). Remove the dough from the refrigerator and divide it into 3 equal parts. Place two in a bowl and cover with a tea towel.

5. Roll the third out to a 9 × 13-inch (23 × 33-cm) rectangle. With the short end facing you, lightly score the dough vertically into three equal parts. Be careful not to completely cut through the dough.

6. Cut ½-inch (12-mm) strips on a slant down each of the outer sections, leaving the middle section intact. Ensure you cut through the dough cleanly.

7. Spread one-third of the filling on the center section of dough.

Continues

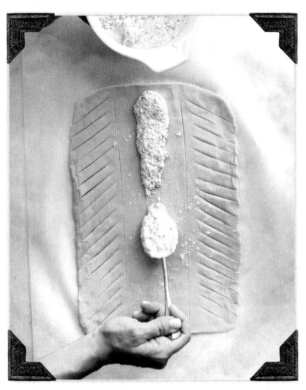

Spread one-third of the filling
on the middle section of dough.

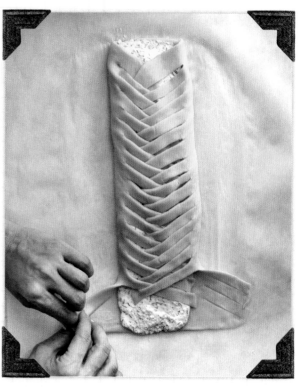

Alternate overlapping the strips
to create a braid down the center.

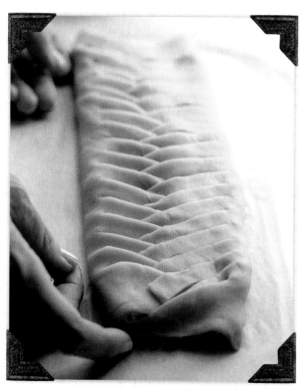

Press the top and bottom pieces
firmly over the filling to seal.

Bake until dark golden brown.

8. Bring the top left strip across the mixture, then overlap with the top right strip. Continue alternating sides to create a braid all the way down the center strip. Press the top and bottom pieces of dough firmly over the filling to seal.

9. Brush the top of the Danish with some of the egg wash, then sprinkle one third of the caraway seeds and salt over the top.

10. Repeat steps 5 through 9 to create 2 more loaves.

11. Place the loaves on a parchment-lined baking sheet, leaving about 3 inches (7.5 cm) between them.

12. Bake for 35 minutes, until dark golden brown. Remove from the oven and transfer to a cooling rack for 15 minutes before serving.

BEA'S WALNUT DANISH

If you have a sweet tooth, make the following ingredient modifications to the main recipe for a tasty walnut treat.

FOR THE DOUGH
Follow the previous recipe, but add 2 tablespoons of sugar instead of ½ teaspoon salt

FOR THE FILLING
Replace the savory cheese filling with the following:

1½ pounds (680 g) ground walnuts (about 6 cups)

1 cup (200 g) sugar

½ cup (120 ml) milk

2 tablespoons bread crumbs

Zest of 1 lemon

2 teaspoons vanilla extract

FOR THE TOPPING
Replace the caraway seeds and salt with 3 tablespoons coarse sugar

BEA PISKER TRIFUNAC

Bea's Burek
(SERBIAN PITA)

serves 6 TO 8 | **PREP** 20 MINUTES | **TOTAL** 1 HOUR AND 5 MINUTES

BUREK, A FAMILY of baked filled pastries made with thin flaky dough, is a popular dish served all over Eastern Europe. The traditional homemade dough bases can be filled with meat or savory and sweet cheeses, and then cut into individual servings and eaten as snacks or hearty lunches. Instead of making the traditional dough used in Serbian bakeries, Nanni Bea makes a home cook's version using phyllo dough (this is also called a "pita," or layered phyllo dish). You can make this recipe with your choice of either meat or cheese filling.

FOR THE MEAT FILLING
1 cup (240 ml) light olive oil

1 small white onion, minced

1 pound (455 g) ground beef, 80 percent lean

½ pound (227 g) ground veal

½ pound (227 g) ground pork

2 teaspoons coarse salt

1 teaspoon freshly ground black pepper

1 large egg beaten with ¼ cup (60 ml) sour cream

FOR THE CHEESE FILLING
4 ounces (115 g) feta cheese, soaked in water overnight

2 pounds (907 g) cottage cheese, strained overnight

½ cup (120 ml) sour cream

5 large eggs, beaten

2 teaspoons coarse salt

¼ cup (30 g) all-purpose flour

FOR ASSEMBLY
1 package phyllo dough, about 25 to 30 sheets

4 large eggs, beaten

1 cup (240 ml) sour cream

½ cup (120 ml) whole milk

1. Preheat the oven to 375°F (190°C).

2. *Prepare the meat filling.* Heat 1 teaspoon of the olive oil over medium heat in a small pan, and cook the onion until it is translucent, about 8 minutes. Set aside to cool.

3. Combine the ground meats, the cooled onion, salt, and the pepper in a large bowl. Add the egg mixture and stir until fully combined.

4. *Alternatively, prepare the cheese filling.* Add the ingredients for the cheese filling to a large bowl and stir until fully combined.

5. *Assemble the pita.* Lightly brush olive oil on the bottom of a 9 × 13-inch (23 × 33-cm) baking pan. Layer 10 phyllo sheets one on top of the other, lightly brushing olive oil between each layer. Spread the filling mixture of your choice on top to fully cover the phyllo.

6. Layer 5 to 6 more sheets of phyllo, brushing oil between each layer, to fully cover the filling.

7. Use a sharp knife to cut 24 squares, cutting all the way to the bottom.

8. Combine the beaten eggs, sour cream, and whole milk and pour this mixture over the pita, spreading it evenly.

9. Bake for 45 minutes, until the topping is golden brown.

Note Pita can be frozen either before or after cooking.

BEA PISKER TRIFUNAC

Bea's Hungarian Paprikash

serves 6 | **PREP** 15 MINUTES | **TOTAL** 1 HOUR AND 30 MINUTES

WHILE PAPRIKASH IS widely eaten in Hungary, it was a staple dish in Bea's mother Greta's Serbian kitchen. Bea loves to add a nice amount of hot paprika for an extra kick, but you can just add a pinch if you prefer yours on the mild side.

4 large tomatoes

2 teaspoons light olive oil

1 (2½ to 3 pound/1.2 to 1.4 kg) whole chicken, cut into 8 pieces

1 large onion, minced

2 red bell peppers, seeded and cut into medium strips

4 teaspoons mild Hungarian paprika

2 pinches hot Hungarian paprika (or to taste)

2 teaspoons Vegeta all-purpose seasoning (optional)

4 teaspoons instant flour (such as Wondra)

1 cup (240 ml) sour cream (optional)

1. Bring a large pot of water to a boil, then drop the whole tomatoes into the water and scald until the skin begins to peel, about 1 minute. Remove from the water. Peel, seed, and chop each tomato into a small dice. Set aside.

2. Heat the olive oil in a large pot over medium heat. Add the chicken and brown on all sides, about 2 minutes per side. Remove from the pan and set aside.

3. Add the onion to the same pot and sauté until translucent. Add the red pepper, diced tomatoes, both paprikas, and Vegeta seasoning and stir to combine. Place the chicken pieces back in the pot. Bring to a boil, then reduce to a simmer, cover, and cook for 45 minutes.

4. Uncover and remove the chicken pieces to a serving dish. Quickly whisk the instant flour into the sauce. Cook 2 more minutes, uncovered.

5. Remove the pot from the heat. Mix in the sour cream (if using; you can also serve alongside) and pour over top of the chicken to serve.

Bea's published chemistry research papers (top) and her old Serbian cookbook (bottom), which she uses regularly to make her favorite recipes.

BEA PISKER TRIFUNAC

Bea's Swedish Palacinka Torta

serves 6 TO 8 | **PREP** 15 MINUTES | **TOTAL** 45 MINUTES

MY CHILDREN, LIKE Bea's, go wild for this unique crepe cake. Each layer of cloudy batter gets quickly cooked in the pan (on one side only) and showered with powdered sugar. Take care to slide each cooked bottom over the uncooked top of the last layer. The heat of the stacked crepes gently cooks the raw, sugared side to create a creamy, light "filling." The final result is a sweet, melt-in-your-mouth crepe cake that will rouse you out of bed in the middle of the night for another bite!

6 large eggs, separated

6 tablespoons (75 g) sugar

6 tablespoons (48 g) all-purpose flour

1 cup (240 ml) whole milk

1 vanilla bean, scraped, or 1 teaspoon vanilla bean paste

1 tablespoon melted butter, cooled

2 to 3 tablespoons olive oil, for pan

3 to 4 cups (375 to 500 g) vanilla confectioners' sugar (recipe at right)

1. Add the egg yolks, sugar, flour, milk, scraped vanilla bean, and melted butter to a large bowl. Mix until fully combined and set aside.

2. In a separate bowl, beat the egg whites with a hand mixer, stand mixer with whisk attachment, or by hand until stiff peaks are formed.

3. Lightly fold the egg whites into the batter until fully combined.

4. Add two teaspoons of olive oil to a 10-inch (25-cm) nonstick pan or crepe pan, and heat over medium heat. Pour about ¼ cup of the batter into the pan. Swirl the pan or spread the batter with the back of a spoon so that the batter thinly covers the entire bottom of the pan. Cook the pancake until it becomes dark golden brown on one side only, about 2 to 3 minutes. Do not flip it over.

5. Gently slide the pancake onto a large cake dish, uncooked side up. Using a mesh strainer, generously dust the top of the pancake with vanilla confectioners' sugar.

6. Repeat the process of cooking, stacking, and sprinkling sugar until the batter is finished. Place the last pancake on the top of the pile, browned side up. Sprinkle the top of the cake with a generous helping of confectioners' sugar.

VANILLA CONFECTIONERS' SUGAR

Add 1 whole vanilla bean to 4 cups confectioners' sugar and mix. Cover and let stand for 3 days before using.

BEA PISKER TRIFUNAC

EUROPE | *Belgrade, Serbia*

Post Card

For Correspondence | Address Only

PART TWO

AFRICA

EGYPT 96 | **GHANA** 103 | **MOROCCO** 106

"Food provides both insight and history of one's culture."

—SAFOI BABANA-HAMPTON

PHYSICAL MAP

OF

AFRICA

English Miles

0 100 200 300 400 500   1000

Below Sea Level
Sea Level – 1,000 feet
1,000 – 2,000 „
2,000 – 5,000 „
5,000 – 10,000 „
Above 10,000 feet „

Africa

Cairo, Egypt

AMINA HEDAYAT

Amina Hedayat grew up in Cairo in a loving family who she credits with instilling in her a strong, independent mind-set.

SHE HAS A DEEP ADMIRATION for her parents, who, regardless of their country's domestic turmoil, endured, prospered, and never allowed Amina to miss a day of school. They experienced times of prosperity and wealth but also times when rationing and frugality were the norm.

At seventeen, Amina married and traveled with her husband to the United States to study. While he worked on his PhD, she began her undergraduate studies at the University of Illinois. From there, she transferred to Michigan State University.

During this time, Amina began a family and raised three boys: Mohammad, Omar, and Yousuf. As a devout Muslim, she found herself troubled by the historical texts her sons were bringing home from grade school. She felt the books were giving a distorted account of Islam, and she feared they were providing her children with a negative perception of Muslims. She discussed her concerns with one of her son's teachers and found the teacher was eager to have Amina share a fair and balanced representation of her culture with the students.

Word spread, and requests for her educational lectures became more frequent. But to speak with confidence and accuracy, Amina knew she needed to study the subject in depth, so she decided to obtain a graduate degree in religious and Islamic studies. She began to lecture to Michigan State students, and her lectures often centered around women and Islam.

Remembering the difficulties of her first days in this new country, Amina also began to assist recent immigrants in her community adapt to their new environment. She helped many women at her mosque obtain drivers' licenses and apply for jobs, and in doing so, she encouraged them to gain a sense of autonomy and self-assurance in a strange place.

Amina's son Mohammad was especially inspired by his mother's strides for religious tolerance and understanding. When he was a boy he did not like to read. But one day, by chance, he decided to leaf through one of the many religious texts his mother had in her eclectic and vast bookcase, and he was hooked. Finally, he had found a subject he could understand and relate to. It was a topic that gave his life meaning, and he credits his own career as a professor of religious studies to his mother's work in religious education.

Today, Amina has parlayed her experience into a new career: She now works as a life coach and mentor to those looking to improve their personal and professional relationships. She hosts workshops and continues to lecture and serve as a consultant. Her ability to guide and educate those in need has served her well—she has helped many people establish and reach their goals. She has spent her life educating others in order to build tolerance across races, and her work as a voice for her culture and beliefs, as well as a champion for other immigrant women, is admirable and inspirational.

Amina's Molokhia Soup

WITH DEMA'A

serves 6 TO 8 | *PREP* 30 MINUTES | *TOTAL* 1 HOUR AND 45 MINUTES

THIS DELICIOUS, HEALTHY soup has always been a staple in Amina's home. Her boys, now grown, still request it when they come to visit. You can find *molokhia* in Middle Eastern markets in the freezer section. It's a vegetable similar in appearance to spinach, but is never eaten raw. The soup of the same name is usually served with rice or flatbread. *Dema'a* is a spiced tomato sauce served alongside the soup. Each guest can pour as little or as much as they like into their bowl.

FOR THE SOUP

2 medium onions

6 tablespoons (89 ml) vegetable oil

2 to 3 balls mastic (Arabic gum)

2 teaspoons ground cardamom

1 (3-pound/1.4-kg) chicken

Coarse salt

Freshly ground black pepper

1 bay leaf

14 ounces (400 g) frozen molokhia

5 garlic cloves, pressed or minced fine

1 teaspoon ground coriander

FOR THE DEMA'A

1 tablespoon vegetable oil

1 tablespoon reserved onion pulp

3 garlic cloves, pressed or minced fine

½ teaspoon ground coriander

¼ teaspoon ground cumin

1 (6-ounce/170 g) can tomato paste

1 (15-ounce/425 g) can tomato sauce

Coarse salt

Freshly ground black pepper

1. Peel the onions and cut them into large chunks. Blend in a food processor for 2 minutes to form a pulp.

2. **Prepare the soup.** Heat 2 tablespoons of the vegetable oil in a large stock pot over medium heat. Add the mastic and ¼ teaspoon of the cardamom and stir to melt the mastic and combine it with the cardamom.

3. Season the chicken with salt and pepper and cover it with the onion pulp, rubbing the onion all over the inside and outside of the skin. Add 2 tablespoons of oil to the pot and sear the chicken on all sides until light brown on the top and bottom, 4 to 5 minutes per side. The onion will fall off the chicken a bit; that's okay.

4. Add about 10 cups (2.4 L) water to the pot to almost completely submerge the chicken.

5. Add the bay leaf and bring the water to a boil. Reduce the heat and cover the pot, leaving the lid ajar so it doesn't boil over, then simmer for 1 hour.

6. Remove the chicken from the pot; reserve the chicken for another use (see Note).

7. Strain the broth through a fine-mesh strainer into a large bowl. Reserve 1 tablespoon of the cooked onion pulp for the dema'a and discard the rest.

8. Return the broth to the pot and bring back to a boil. Reduce to a simmer, add the frozen molokhia, and cover with the lid. Make sure the broth does not return to a boil.

9. Heat the remaining 2 tablespoons of the oil over low heat in a small sauté pan.

10. Add the garlic and cook for 1 minute, careful not to brown.

11. Add the coriander and cook for 1 more minute, just until the garlic starts to brown slightly.

12. Remove the lid from the soup and add the garlic-coriander oil. Season to taste with salt and pepper. The molokhia should be broken down and cooked through. Remove from the heat, cover, and set aside.

13. ***Prepare the dema'a.*** Combine the oil and reserved onion pulp in a small saucepan and heat over medium heat. When hot, add the garlic, coriander, and cumin. Reduce to low and cook for 2 to 3 minutes, until the garlic softens enough to be incorporated with the other ingredients.

14. Add the tomato paste, tomato sauce, and 2 cups (480 ml) water. Bring to a boil, then reduce to a simmer, cover, and simmer for 10 minutes. Season with salt and pepper to taste.

15. Ladle the soup into bowls and top with 2 to 3 teaspoons of the dema'a, or more, to taste.

Note

Amina likes to use every portion of her ingredients, opting to serve the chicken that's left over from making the broth beside the soup. Once she removes it from the cooking liquid, she brushes it with tomato paste and broils it to get a nice, crispy finish. Personally, I like to just shred the chicken and add it to the soup.

Amina's Koshary

serves — 4 TO 6 | **PREP** 45 MINUTES | **TOTAL** 1 HOUR

ON THE STREETS of Cairo, little carts are set up with all the components of this tasty rice bowl and when you order, the layers are scooped together for a delicious flavor combination. To recreate this at home, set the individual dishes out for each person to assemble their own bowl as they like. My food stylist and wildly talented chef, Alexandra, deep-fried the onions to get them extra crispy like the ones in Cairo.

FOR THE LENTILS

1 cup (190 g) black or brown lentils

2 teaspoons coarse salt, divided

FOR THE CRISPY FRIED ONIONS

1 cup (240 ml) vegetable oil

1 large onion, sliced thin

FOR THE RICE

1 cup (200 g) white rice (short grain), rinsed and drained

1 teaspoon coarse salt

FOR THE PASTA

1 cup (112 g) ditalini pasta

1 tablespoon olive oil

2 teaspoons coarse salt

FOR THE CHICKPEAS

1 (15-ounce/430 g) can chickpeas, drained

1 teaspoon coarse salt

FOR THE DEMA'A

1 tablespoon vegetable oil

1 tablespoon finely minced onion

3 garlic cloves, pressed or minced fine

½ teaspoon ground coriander

¼ teaspoon ground cumin

1 (6-ounce/170 g) can tomato paste

1 (15-ounce/425 g) can tomato sauce

Coarse salt

Freshly ground black pepper

Hot red pepper sauce (optional, for serving)

1. *Make the lentils.* Add the lentils and enough water to cover to a small saucepan. Add 1 teaspoon of the salt and bring to a boil. Then reduce to a simmer and cook according to the package instructions until the lentils puff and soften, about 45 minutes. Drain and set aside.

2. *While the lentils are cooking, make the fried onions.* Heat the oil to 350°F (175°C) in a medium saucepan and carefully drop in the onion slices. Gently stir with a large slotted spoon to separate the slices. Cook, stirring, until the ends are very crisp and the onions are deep brown. Remove to paper towels to drain and set aside. Reserve the cooking oil.

3. *Make the rice.* Cook the rice as per the package instructions. Set aside.

4. *Make the pasta.* Cook the pasta as per the package instructions. Drain and toss with the olive oil and salt and set aside.

5. Place 2 tablespoons of the oil used to cook the onions in a medium sauté pan. Add the lentils to the pan with the remaining 1 teaspoon salt and cook, stirring, over medium heat until they begin to brown, about 5 minutes. Remove from the heat immediately and fold into the cooked rice.

6. *Make the chickpeas.* Heat the chickpeas, the remaining reserved onion oil, and the salt in a medium sauté pan over medium heat until heated through.

7. Prepare the dema'a following the instructions on page 99. To serve, set out all of the dishes so each person can assemble their own bowl as follows: Start with the rice and lentil mixture as a base. Then add chickpeas, pasta, and crispy onions. Finish with a dollop of the dema'a and some hot sauce if desired.

Amina's Fattah

serves 6 | PREP 15 MINUTES | TOTAL 1 HOUR

AMINA JOKES THAT Egyptians truly love their carbohydrates! This savory lamb dish is served over rice with a crispy bed of pita bread underneath. The punch from the tomato-vinegar sauce gets soaked up by all the rice and pita for a delicious explosion of flavor. This is a hearty, comforting dish, perfect for a cold winter night.

½ cup (120 ml) vegetable oil

3 balls mastic (Arabic gum)

¼ teaspoon cardamom

1 pound (455 g) lamb stew meat, cut into 2-inch (5-cm) chunks

Coarse salt

Freshly ground black pepper

1 bay leaf

1 cup (200 g) short-grain white rice (Amina prefers Calrose)

2 whole rounds white pita bread, cut into small pieces

3 garlic cloves, pressed or minced

2 tablespoons white vinegar

1 (15-ounce/425 g) can tomato sauce

1 large onion, thinly sliced

1. Heat 3 teaspoons of the vegetable oil in a large pot over medium heat. Add the mastic and cardamom and stir gently to melt the mastic.

2. Add the lamb and season with 1 teaspoon each of salt and pepper. Brown the meat for 3 to 5 minutes on each side.

3. Add the bay leaf to the pot along with enough water to cover the meat, 2 to 3 cups (480 to 720 ml). Bring to a boil, then reduce to a simmer and cook until the meat is fork-tender, 40 to 45 minutes. Remove from the heat.

4. While the meat cooks, prepare the rice according to the package instructions and set aside, covered, to keep warm.

5. Heat 3 teaspoons of the vegetable oil in a medium sauté pan over medium heat. Add the pieces of pita bread and fry until golden and crisp, 2 to 3 minutes (see Note). Remove to paper towels to drain. Combine the toasted pita with ½ cup (120 ml) of the cooking liquid from the lamb in a large bowl to soften the bread. Set aside.

6. Heat 2 teaspoons of the vegetable oil in a small saucepan over low heat. Add the garlic and cook, just until the garlic begins to brown, about 3 minutes. Add the vinegar and tomato sauce. Season with salt and pepper to taste and simmer for 10 minutes.

7. While the sauce cooks, heat the remaining vegetable oil in a large frying pan over high heat, then add the onions and cook until they are dark and crispy, about 10 minutes.

8. Place the softened pita in an even layer on the bottom of a large casserole dish or serving platter. Spread the cooked rice on top to create a second layer. Drain the lamb and layer the meat on top of the rice. Spoon the tomato sauce all over the meat. Top with the crispy onions and serve.

Note

Instead of frying the bread, sometimes Amina will toast it for a lighter option. To toast in the oven, heat at 350°F (175°C) for 10 minutes, flipping the pieces at the 5-minute mark.

JENNIPHER AGYEMANG

◆

WHEN JENNIPHER AGYEMANG WAS YOUNG, her mother, Akosua, would cook daily for the entire family. Her kitchen was the nucleus around which Jennipher and her siblings revolved. Until very recently, her mother would only eat food she had prepared herself, and Jennipher now feels the same way about her own cooking. For her, home-cooked Ashanti food is the only food she desires to eat, and nothing makes her happier than a big pot of her own fish soup (page 104).

For Jennipher, the hardest part of leaving West Africa to give her daughter a better life and a chance at an education was leaving her family behind. For Ghanaians, "family" has a very broad, inclusive definition. Your family isn't just your mother, father, and siblings. Instead, your family is a special tribe of individuals, a group of people who work together every day for the common good of the whole community.

This sense of extended family upbringing contributes greatly to how close Jennipher is with her daughter, Candace, and her grandsons. To support Candace, she makes sure her growing grandsons are safe and happy, whether cradled in her arms or wrapped in a large cloth nestled on her back (their preferred way to fall asleep). She is with her grandsons every day while her daughter works, and she cooks them her cherished family recipes and speaks to them in Twi so that they can be acquainted with their native culture. As with many Ashantis, Jennipher believes her grandchildren are her children, too—there is no difference between a mother's child and grandchild.

Taking care of others is Jennipher's greatest gift, and she relishes giving her care and attention to her loved ones. While Ghana will always be her homeland, home is where her family is.

Jennipher's Ashanti Fish Soup

serves 6 | **PREP** 20 MINUTES | **TOTAL** 2 HOURS

SOUPS AND STEWS are very important to the Ghanaian diet. In fact, Jennipher explained that Ashanti babies begin to eat soup at just five months old. For a traditional version of this soup, you must use garden eggs (small, eggplant-like vegetables), which Jennipher brings back from each of her visits home and then freezes for future dishes. Smoked fish is common in Ghanaian soups and stews, giving the broth a very deep flavor.

1½-inch (4-cm) piece ginger

½ garlic clove

1 large white onion

1 (2 to 3 pound/907 g to 1.4 kg) whole red snapper

3 red onions

3 plum tomatoes

1 fish bouillon cube (Jennipher prefers Maggi, crayfish flavor)

1 (2 to 3 pound/907 g to 1.4 kg) whole smoked catfish, skin removed

1 (8-ounce/227 g) can tomato sauce

¼ cup (60 ml) African garden eggs (boiled then frozen), rinsed

12 ounces (340 g) wild oyster mushrooms, peeled and cut into 1-inch (2.5-cm) pieces

2 teaspoons salt, plus more to taste

1. Preheat the oven to 400°F (205°C).

2. Puree the ginger, garlic, and white onion in a food processor. Set aside.

3. Remove any scales from the fish, then rub it with the onion mixture.

4. Lightly oil a baking sheet or line it with parchment. Place the fish on the baking sheet and bake for 45 minutes. Set aside to cool.

5. Heat 8 cups (2 L) water in a medium stockpot over medium-high heat.

6. Mince one red onion, quarter the second, and leave the third one whole.

7. Add the minced red onion, whole red onion, and tomatoes to the pot. Bring to a boil, then add the bouillon and smoked catfish. Boil rapidly for 10 minutes.

8. Remove the tomatoes and the whole red onion, and puree them in a blender with 2 tablespoons of the cooking liquid. Add about ¾ of the tomato puree to the pot along with the can of tomato sauce.

9. Puree the garden eggs, the quartered red onion, and the remaining ¼ of the tomato puree in the blender until smooth. Add the puree to the soup.

10. Add the mushrooms and salt to the pot and boil for 10 more minutes.

11. Cut the baked fish into three or four pieces (head, body, and tail) and add it to the soup. Jennipher saves the head for herself!

12. Boil for 10 more minutes. Taste for salt and add more if needed. Serve over Fufu (opposite).

Jennipher's Fufu

GHANAIANS LOVE THEIR fufu! A staple food in the Ghanaian diet, fufu is made by pounding cassava and unripe plantains into a fine powder, and then mixing it with water to create a soft, pliable dough. The round dough is the perfect accompaniment to many of the soups and stews that are the backbone of Ghanaian food. Jennipher's mother would use a large wooden mortar with a heavy wooden pestle to grind the plantain and cassava into a fine flour for the fufu base, but here in the States, many home cooks (Jennipher included) skip this step and purchase pre-ground fufu mix. To make it extra tasty, Jennipher adds an additional fresh plantain and uses a pestle to bring the dough together before serving.

1 green plantain, peeled and diced

2 cups (454 g) powdered Fufu mix (Jennipher prefers Mama's Choice)

1. Heat the fresh plantain with enough water to cover in a medium stockpot over medium-high heat. Bring to a boil, cover, and cook until the plantain is fork-tender, 7 minutes. Reserve the liquid.

2. Drain, then puree the plantain in a blender, adding cooking liquid as necessary to make a smooth sauce. Add the fufu mix and blend until a thick paste forms. Add more cooking liquid as needed to incorporate and fully mix the powder and plantain.

3. Discard any remaining cooking liquid and pour the blended mixture back into the pot. Turn the heat to low.

4. Add enough water to cover the paste and stir to incorporate the water and thin the mixture. Cook, stirring, for 4 minutes until all the water is incorporated.

5. Then, add more water to just cover the mixture, cover, increase the heat to medium-high, and boil for 4 more minutes.

6. Remove the lid and stir until all the water is incorporated and the fufu begins to pull away from the sides of the pot. It will take 3 to 4 minutes of stirring to create a pliable dough.

7. Place the fufu with a bit of water in a low, shallow bowl.

8. Using a large wooden pestle, press into the fufu to smooth it out. Wet the pestle every few minutes with running water, and press into the fufu until the mixture is completely smooth and all of the water has been incorporated.

9. Wet your hands and pull the outer edges of the fufu toward the middle to form a large ball.

10. Carefully lift the fufu and flip it over. Tear off small pieces and roll into balls about 3 inches in diameter.

11. Place a ball of the fufu in a bowl, ladle a stew, saucey dish, or soup (such as Jennipher's Ashanti Fish Soup, opposite) around the fufu, and enjoy immediately.

→ Jennipher and her daughter, Candace, Christmas 1999.

SAFOI BABANA-HAMPTON

SAFOI CAME TO THE UNITED STATES as a Fulbright fellow. She enrolled in a graduate program at Indiana University, where she earned an MA in Comparative Literature, then went on to pursue a PhD in Modern French Studies at the University of Maryland, College Park, a subject she now teaches at Michigan State University.

Morocco was a French protectorate until the mid-1950s. To this day, French is one of the main languages spoken there (along with Arabic and Berber), and a second language for many Moroccans. As her academic research is primarily in the areas of twentieth-century and contemporary French and Francophone cultural studies, these areas of research and teaching converge with elements of her cultural heritage. Most recently, Safoi's scholarly work was recognized internationally when she led the production of the two documentary films *Hmong Memory at the Crossroads* (2015) and *Growing up Hmong at the Crossroads* (2017).

Safoi has always worked to find a balance between immersing herself in American culture and her studies while, at the same time, maintaining strong ties with her native culture and way of life. Passing on her Moroccan culture to her two children, Malek and Sarah, is extremely important to her. Her home is filled with artifacts from her homeland that carry historical significance or spiritual value. She also makes sure to celebrate Moroccan cooking traditions with her children. As Safoi explains, "Food provides both insight and history of one's culture."

Safoi's Kaab el Ghazal

("GAZELLE HORN" ALMOND COOKIES)

makes 20 | **PREP** 20 MINUTES | **TOTAL** 1 HOUR AND 45 MINUTES

THESE DELICIOUS HORN-SHAPED almond cookies, called *kaab el ghazal*, are the most common Moroccan dessert. Afternoon tea in Morocco is a daily ritual, and Safoi explained that these almond cookies are often eaten alongside mint tea.

1½ cups (175 g) almond meal

½ cup (100 g) sugar

11 tablespoons (151 g) unsalted butter, melted

2 tablespoons orange flower water

2 cups (250 g) all-purpose flour

1 large egg

Pinch of salt

1. Line a baking sheet with parchment paper and set aside.

2. Combine the almond meal, sugar, 3 tablespoons of the butter, and the orange flower water in a medium bowl to create an almond paste. Set aside.

3. Combine the flour, egg, remaining butter, and salt in a food processor until a smooth dough forms. Divide the dough in half.

4. Knead one half until it is soft and pliable, 2 to 3 minutes. Roll out the dough on a piece of parchment paper to ¼ inch (6 mm) thick. Using a 3-inch (7.5-cm) biscuit cutter or a drinking glass, cut out circles from the dough, rerolling the scraps to use all of the dough. You will have about 10 circles.

5. Repeat with the remaining dough. You will have about 20 circles total.

6. Place about 1 teaspoon of almond paste on each round of pastry dough and fold the dough to encase the filling. Seal the edges to form a crescent or horn shape.

7. Place the cookies on the prepared pan. Let them rest for 1 hour before baking.

8. Preheat the oven to 350°F (175°C). Bake the cookies for 20 to 25 minutes, until light golden brown.

Safoi's Chicken Tagine

serves 6 | **PREP** 25 MINUTES | **TOTAL** 1 HOUR AND 25 MINUTES

SAFOI HAS MANY beautiful tagines in her home in Michigan. A tagine is a cooking vessel used in many Moroccan recipes that's made of earthenware and has a domed top that returns all condensation to the food, keeping everything moist (genius!). It is perfect for slow-cooked foods. Stews and bone-in chicken dishes are created in this beautiful pot, and the flavor is unmatched. Meat falls off the bone and all the flavors marry together. If you invest in one, you may never use your slow cooker again.

Tagine is also the name of a type of dish commonly served in Morocco. A tagine is a slow-cooked savory and hearty stew that is made in the pot of the same name. If you already own a slow cooker, you don't necessarily have to buy a tagine (see Note). But when I place my tagine on the stove and fire it up, I feel as if I've been transported to Morocco.

FOR THE MARINADE

½ teaspoon saffron threads

1 teaspoon ground ginger

1 tablespoon coarse salt

1 teaspoon freshly ground black pepper

½ cup (120 ml) extra-virgin olive oil

½ cup (120 ml) canola oil

FOR THE STEW

1 (1½-pound/1.7 kg) whole chicken

7 large carrots, peeled

1 small yellow onion, minced

½ cup (75 g) olives (Mediterranean or Kalamata)

½ preserved lemon, sliced thin

1 tablespoon parsley, chopped

1. Combine the saffron, ginger, salt, pepper, olive oil, and canola oil in a large bowl. Set aside.

2. Clean and thoroughly wash the chicken, then cut it into 8 pieces.

3. Add the chicken to the bowl with the marinade, massaging the marinade into the chicken.

4. Cut the carrots in half and remove their yellow cores.

5. Open the tagine and lay the onion on the bottom. Arrange the carrots over the onion.

6. Lay the chicken with all of the marinade over the vegetables. Add 1 cup (240 ml) water and cover.

7. Cook on very low heat for 1 hour. Check at the 30-minute mark to ensure the bottom is not dry. Add another ½ cup (120 ml) water if necessary.

8. In the last 5 minutes of cooking, add the olives and the preserved lemon.

9. Garnish with parsley to serve.

Note

To make this recipe in a slow cooker, follow the directions through step 7, and set the slow cooker on high for 4 hours. Add the olives and lemon at the 3-hour-and-45-minute mark.

SAFOI BABANA-HAMPTON

"Home cooks
always cook
with their
heart and
soul, and that
is universal."
—DAISY CHOY

TINA HSIA YAO

Tina Yao was born in a war zone in 1942.

THE DAUGHTER OF A MAJOR general for the Chinese Nationalist Party, the first few years of her life were spent moving from place to place, constantly on the run for safety. When she was seven, her family had no choice but to flee their home in Sichuan, China, and relocate to the island of Taiwan.

Before graduating with a degree in Chinese literature in Taiwan, she married her husband, William, an accountant for Pan America in the United States. After graduation, she moved to the United States with him and settled into a new life in Queens, New York. Soon after arriving, she began working toward obtaining another degree, this time in secondary education. A college degree was a priority for her: She wanted to model the importance of education to her children, despite the challenges of obtaining a degree in a foreign language and system.

The turmoil of Tina's childhood seems to have shaped her into a woman who doesn't waste time. Always seeking progress and betterment, she found herself unfulfilled by office work and instead began buying a number of businesses. She owned a real estate firm and dabbled in the restaurant industry—at one point, she even owned a pizzeria. She was always willing to take on a new investment, manage success, and then move on to the next opportunity. Her children, Nancy and James, both recognize how driven their mother has always been, putting her true loves—literature, poetry, and art—aside to pursue avenues that would provide better models for them.

Interestingly, her daughter feels her mother's true identity manifests in her cooking. When Tina prepares food, it is with intention and an artist's eye. To watch Tina make dumplings (page 115) is to see a true art form. Her fingers, quick and nimble, create uniform, perfect pleats on every identical piece. She patiently lines up the beautiful purses—almost too beautiful to eat—until there are rows of hundreds. Then she carefully drops them into the boiling water, gingerly swirling the water with her chopsticks until they plump to the surface, ready for her family to devour.

Now retired, Tina spends her days attending art and pottery classes, writing poetry, and spending time with her grandchildren (and she still flips investment properties!). Nancy is convinced if her mother hadn't always been so ambitious about achieving the "American dream," she would have been a celebrated artist or poet. Instead, Tina worked tirelessly to provide opportunities for her children. Working hard to get what you want out of life is very important to Tina, and she feels Chinese people are instilled with a determined work ethic from a very young age.

Tina looks to philosophy for daily guidance. Ever since she was a child, she has studied many Chinese philosophers, and she relies on their teachings to get her through difficult periods in her life. She feels particularly drawn to a quote from Confucius: "To put the world right in order, we must first put the nation in order; to put the nation in order, we must first put the family in order; to put the family in order, we must first cultivate our personal life; we must first set our hearts right." Simply put by Tina, "Put my heart in the right place, then I can serve my family, then my country, and then I can change the world!" Her words, her food, and her outlook on life all fit together in perfect harmony.

A photograph of Tina and her family celebrating Chinese New Year, circa 1960 (Tina is third from left).

Tina's Nian Gao

(CHINESE NEW YEAR CAKE)

makes TWO 6-INCH (15-CM) ROUND CAKES | *PREP* 20 MINUTES | *TOTAL* 1 HOUR AND 5 MINUTES

ALONG WITH DUMPLINGS (opposite), Tina always makes *nian gao*, a sticky dessert traditionally eaten for Chinese New Year. Tina explained that it is eaten to celebrate the new year because the words *nian* and *gao* literally translate to "sticky cake," but they also have a very similar sound to the words for "higher" and "year." Hence, the Chinese believe that eating it during a new year celebration will guarantee an elevated status in the upcoming year. There are many variations of this cake throughout China. Tina makes two kinds, one with red bean paste and the other with walnuts, and this recipe will give you a little of both. They are always decorated with six dried red dates because the number six represents life going smoothly.

2¼ cups (360 g) glutinous rice flour

¾ cup (180 ml) warm water

¾ cup (165 g) packed brown sugar

1½ cups (360 ml) red bean paste

1 cup (120 g) chopped walnuts

12 dried red dates, rinsed

2 tablespoons unsalted butter, softened

1. Place the flour, water, and brown sugar in a large bowl. With a hand or stand mixer, beat on medium until all the ingredients are combined and a thick batter forms. Remove half of the batter to another bowl.

2. Add the red bean paste to the first bowl and mix until combined.

3. Add the walnuts to the second bowl and mix until combined.

4. Butter two 6-inch (15-cm) round aluminum pans and pour one bowl of batter into each. Place the pans in a steamer (Tina uses a large double steamer where the cake can rest in the steaming basket), cover, and cook for 45 minutes. They are ready when a cake tester comes out clean.

5. Carefully tip the pans to remove any condensation from the tops of the cakes.

6. Let the cakes cool and firm up completely while in the pans, about 15 minutes.

7. Cut into squares while still in the pan and serve warm. For another traditional preparation, cut the cake into thin slices, dip each slice in egg white, and fry with a tablespoon of neutral oil in a medium pan over medium heat until crispy.

TINA HSIA YAO

TINA'S CHINESE NEW YEAR
Dumplings

serves 8 TO 10 (MAKES 80 DUMPLINGS) | *PREP* 35 MINUTES | *TOTAL* 1 HOUR 20 MINUTES

WHEAT IS A staple crop in the northern region of China, so the cuisine of the north is known for dumplings and noodle dishes. In Tina's village, the women would sit for hours making these dumplings in preparation for the new year, eating and gossiping as they worked. Tina makes her thin dumpling skins with just two ingredients: flour and water. Then she stuffs each skin with a savory pork filling that she mixes up with chopsticks, and she seals each one with perfect, identical pleats in the blink of an eye. Tina's secret for super-moist dumplings is her addition of soft tofu. She feels pork here in the United States is too lean, so she adds the tofu to soften the filling and give it a juicier bite.

This recipe takes a bit of elbow grease, but if you are simply serving it as an appetizer, you'll be left with plenty of extra that you can pop in the freezer. They are so delicious and versatile—try them steamed, fried, or even boiled in your favorite soup!

FOR THE DOUGH
4 cups (500 g) all-purpose flour, plus more for dusting

1 cup (240 ml) warm water

FOR THE FILLING
1 head Napa cabbage

1 pound (455 g) ground pork

¼ cup (60 g) minced soft tofu

2 tablespoons minced ginger

2 scallions, thinly sliced

1 tablespoon soy sauce, plus more for serving

2 tablespoons white wine

FOR SERVING
Soy sauce

Hot chili oil

1. **Make the dough.** Place the flour in a large bowl and create a well in the center. Pour the water into the well, then, with your hands, incorporate the flour with the water and knead until a ball forms. Continue kneading for 20 minutes, until the dough is perfectly smooth and round. Allow the dough to rest, covered, for 30 minutes.

2. **Make the filling.** Slice the cabbage thinly. Combine the cabbage with cold water to cover in a large pot. Bring to a boil over high heat and cook until the cabbage is soft, 5 to 10 minutes. Drain and let cool.

3. Combine the cabbage with the pork, tofu, ginger, scallions, soy sauce, and white wine in a large bowl.

4. **Assemble the dumplings.** Flour your work space and two sheet pans. Cut the dough into 4 equal pieces. Keep 3 pieces covered with plastic wrap while working with the fourth. Use your hands to roll one piece into a log about 1 inch (2.5 cm) in diameter and 20 inches (50 cm) long. Pinch off 1-inch (2.5-cm) pieces and flatten each with the palm of your hand. You should have 20 pieces.

Continues

Place 1 teaspoon of the filling in the center
of the dough circle and fold in half.

Pinch the edges together into small pleats
between your thumbs and forefingers.

Continue until the edges are fully sealed.

Practice makes perfect!

5. Use a rolling pin (a short, thin rolling pin is best) to roll out the edges of the dough to about 3 inches (7.5 cm) in diameter. Place 1 teaspoon of the filling in the center and fold in half, encasing the filling, then pinch the edges together until fully sealed—practice makes perfect! Place the dumplings on the prepared baking sheets.

6. Repeat with the remaining dough and filling to make approximately 80 dumplings.

7. Boil a large pot of water and drop in 10 to 15 dumplings at a time. Cook until they rise to the top, 5 to 7 minutes.

8. Serve with soy sauce and hot chili oil to taste.

TINA HSIA YAO

DAISY CHOY

◆

DAISY CHOY WAS RAISED IN Hong Kong and didn't really believe she would ever leave. She married, became a teacher, and was raising her small children, Vicky and Eric, when her husband Dennis's career in commerce provided the opportunity to begin life anew—in 1984, the family made plans to move to New York. Upon hearing this exciting news, Daisy enrolled in Mrs. Lucy Lo's traditional Chinese cooking class at Town Gas Center in Hong Kong to hone her culinary skills before leaving home.

Becoming a talented chef might just have been in her DNA: Daisy's ancestors are from Shun Tak County of Guangdong Province, which is very well known for its cooking. When people eat in Hong Kong restaurants, they will ask, "Is this dish from Shun Tak?" This question is complimentary, because the food of Shun Tak is known for being fresh, light, and delicious. Daisy recounts how the unmarried, older women who lived there devoted their lives to cooking and weaving. These recipes, passed down through the generations, are highly revered in Hong Kong and throughout China.

When they first arrived in the United States, Daisy chose to stay at home with her children to help them acclimate to their new life. She knew living in America would expose her children to new people, and she was excited by that prospect. Before she enrolled her son, Eric, in kindergarten, she decided to teach him English. When she informed him, he refused, saying "You are my momma and you will only speak to me in Chinese. I will learn English in school!"

At first, Daisy was concerned, but after some research she found that speaking one's mother tongue at home is very comforting to young children: It reassures them that everything is going to be the same regardless of their new surroundings and gives them a safe haven within a new place. In the fall, her children started school and quickly learned English, but to this day, they speak with their mother only in Cantonese.

Currently, Daisy resides in a small suburb of San Francisco and works with small children as a speech pathologist. The food Daisy prepares is unmistakably Chinese, but it's much more refined, simple, and delicate than what you would find on a typical Chinese restaurant menu in the United States. Daisy said she was thrilled to be part of this collection because "home cooks always cook with their heart and soul, and that is universal."

Daisy's Winter Melon Soup

serves — 6 AS FIRST COURSE | PREP 15 MINUTES | TOTAL 1 HOUR

TRUE CANTONESE COOKING is very light: It relies on soups, steamed fish, pork, and vegetables. Despite what its name implies, in China this soup is commonly served in the summer, when winter melon is in season. Southern Chinese typically eat soup at every dinner. It is served first while the main course is still cooking. This soup is traditionally flavored with lotus leaf (which is discarded before serving), but Daisy has omitted it here because she often can't find it locally.

1½ pounds (680 g) winter melon, peeled, seeded, and cut into 1-inch (2.5-cm) dice

1-inch (2.5-cm) piece organic ginger, sliced thin with skin on

5 dried scallops, soaked overnight and shredded

1 (¼-pound/115 g) chicken breast, cut into small pieces

5 medium shrimp, peeled, deveined, and cut into small pieces

Soy sauce or salt, to taste

1. Bring 6 cups (1.4 L) water to a boil in a large pot. Add the winter melon, ginger, and dried scallops. Return to a boil, then reduce to a simmer and cook for 15 to 20 minutes.

2. Add the chicken breast and simmer for 10 to 15 minutes, adding the shrimp in the last 3 minutes of cooking.

3. Season with soy sauce to taste. Serve warm or at room temperature.

DAISY CHOY

Daisy's Steamed Fish

serves 2 TO 4 | PREP 10 MINUTES | TOTAL 25 TO 35 MINUTES

DAISY EXPLAINED THAT the Chinese look to food for its medicinal qualities and eat particular dishes at certain times of their lives. For example, after a woman gives birth, the baby's grandmother will make a black vinegar stew for the mother that has pork feet, for their calcium, and ginger, for its anti-inflammatory properties, which she will eat daily for a month after the baby is born. While preparing this fish dish, Daisy spoke about how important fish was to her family's diet. Growing up close to the South China Sea, they had regular access to fresh fish. This dish is healthy, light, and uses ginger and scallion as the star ingredients in the simple sauce. While the fish can be fried in peanut oil, Daisy prefers it steamed to make it that much healthier.

FOR THE FISH

1 pound (455 g) white fish fillets of your choice (Daisy prefers grouper, snapper, sole, or turbo)

1 teaspoon ground ginger

1 teaspoon white pepper

1 teaspoon cornstarch

3 scallions, white parts only (reserve greens for sauce)

1-inch (2.5-cm) piece fresh ginger cut into thin strips, skin on

1 to 2 tablespoons peanut oil

FOR THE SAUCE

2 tablespoons peanut oil

2-inch (5-cm) piece fresh ginger, peeled and cut into matchsticks

3 scallions, green parts only, sliced very thin, crosswise (about ½ cup/30 g)

1 tablespoon soy sauce

1 teaspoon sesame oil

FOR SERVING

Cooked white rice (Daisy prefers Kokuho Rose brand)

1. *Prepare the fish.* Clean and dry the fillets thoroughly. Sprinkle the ground ginger, white pepper, and cornstarch onto both sides of the fish and rub in. Set aside.

2. Pour enough water to come one-quarter of the way up the sides of a large skillet and bring to a boil over high heat.

3. Cut the whites of the scallions into long strips and place them on a thin dish or steamer rack, reserving 3 to 4 pieces. Place the fish on top of the scallions, then place the reserved scallions and sliced ginger on top. Drizzle the fish with peanut oil. Cover with parchment paper.

4. Place the dish holding the prepared fish in the skillet, cover, and steam until the fish is cooked through, flaky, and fully opaque (as little as 8 minutes for delicate fillets like sole, or up to 12 minutes for a dense fish like grouper).

5. *Prepare the sauce.* Heat the peanut oil in a medium saucepan over high heat. When the oil begins to shimmer, turn the heat down to medium-low and add the ginger and scallion greens. Cook until tender, 3 to 5 minutes.

6. Add the soy sauce, sesame oil, and 1 tablespoon water. Cook for 5 minutes, until all is heated through.

7. Remove the pieces of scallion and ginger that steamed with the fish and discard. Place the fish on a serving platter and drizzle the sauce over the top. Serve with white rice.

SOON SUN KANG HUH

WHEN SOON SUN KANG HUH'S children come home to visit, they know they can find her in the kitchen making something delicious. Whether it's the traditional Korean dishes they grew up eating for dinner or American fare like lasagna, everyone knows she cooks enough to send all three home with neatly packed leftovers.

Soon Sun was born in Seoul, South Korea, shortly after her family emigrated from Pyongyang, North Korea, before the start of the Korean War. The youngest daughter in her family, Soon spent much of her time in the kitchen learning her mother's traditional dishes from the North, which Soon felt tended to be less salty and spicy than Southern food. She has always had a deep love for cooking, and it's one of the countless ways she expresses her love for her family and friends.

As her daughter Gabrielle explains, Soon Sun may be petite in frame and delicate in appearance, but she is the true force of her family. She immigrated to the United States with her husband, Chan Woo, and eldest daughter, Grace, in June 1976, and her husband's job as a medical doctor led the family to many new places, from Brooklyn to Boston (where her son, Timothy, was born) to Oklahoma, Pennsylvania, and New Jersey, where she now resides with her husband. Despite being limited in English, especially after first moving to America, Soon Sun always embraced change and managed to create a loving home wherever the family landed. She also embraced American food, so spaghetti and meatballs, meatloaf, and homemade cinnamon rolls were regulars in the Huh household. Looking back, her daughter knows her mother must have been scared in the beginning, especially because of the language barrier and being so far from her family, but she never let that deter her and always forged ahead to make the best life for her family.

Soon is incredibly spiritual, and her faith is an integral part of her life—prayer and being an active member of her church community are important to her. Her food carries an impressive level of precision and passion. When cooking in traditional Korean fashion, Soon is undeterred by the extra pans and time it takes, because she wants to ensure each ingredient maintains not only its color but also its taste. Her love of God, family, and food is infused into her cooking, and it's this quality that makes each of her dishes carry so much significance with her children and grandchildren.

Soon's Bibimbap

(EGG AND VEGETABLE RICE BOWL)

serves 6 | *PREP* 45 MINUTES | *TOTAL* 2 HOURS

WHEN PREPARING THIS well-known Korean dish, I urge you to take the time to follow the Korean cooking practice. The ingredients are respected and cooked separately in order to honor color and taste. By taking the time to cook them separately, the flavors are not muddied before composing the final dish. Each ingredient carries its own distinct flavor, and when you are eating the dish, they come together perfectly under a delicious sunny-side-up egg. The bed of rice provides a wonderful place for the runny yolk to rest, creating a creamy base for all the meat and vegetables.

½ pound (227 g) beef tenderloin, thinly sliced into strips

2 tablespoons sesame oil

3 tablespoons soy sauce

1 tablespoon plus ¼ teaspoon minced garlic

Freshly ground black pepper

1½ ounces (3-ounce/85-g package) dried bellflower root (also known as platycodon)

Coarse salt

3 to 4 tablespoons grapeseed oil, plus more if needed

1¼ teaspoons crushed roasted sesame seeds

1 to 2 zucchini (about ½ pound/227 g), thinly sliced

1 tablespoon plus ¼ teaspoon sugar

1 bunch (8 ounces/227 g) fresh Korean spinach or large leaf/regular spinach

2 tablespoons chopped scallion

½ cup (7-ounce/200 g) royal fern (a shoot commonly found in Korean markets)

½ pound (227 g) shiitake mushrooms, thinly sliced

1 to 2 carrots (about ½ pound/227 g), julienned (matchstick size) and lightly salted

3 tablespoons gochujang (spicy red pepper paste)

Cooked white rice

6 large eggs

1. Combine the sliced beef, 1 tablespoon of the sesame oil, 2 tablespoons of the soy sauce, 1½ teaspoons of the minced garlic, and ½ teaspoon pepper in a medium bowl or plastic storage bag. Refrigerate while preparing the rest of the ingredients. Can be made ahead the night before.

2. Add the bellflower root to a medium bowl and cover with 2 cups (480 ml) cold water. Let sit for 2 hours, rinse, and then drain. Split the root into matchstick-size pieces, rub the pieces with 2 teaspoons salt, and let stand for 10 minutes to remove the bitterness. Rinse thoroughly with cold water to remove excess salt. Drain and set aside.

3. Sauté the bellflower root with 1 tablespoon of the grapeseed oil and a pinch of salt over medium heat until soft, about 20 minutes. Stir in ½ teaspoon of the sesame seeds. Set aside.

Continues

4. Toss the zucchini with ½ teaspoon salt and let sit for 30 minutes. Lightly squeeze to remove excess water. Sauté the zucchini with 1 teaspoon of the grapeseed oil, ¼ teaspoon each of the sugar, salt, garlic, and sesame seeds. Set aside.

5. Bring a pot of water to a boil and prepare an ice water bath. In small batches, dunk the spinach in the boiling water for 30 seconds, then shock in the ice water bath and squeeze out excess water. Toss with 1 teaspoon of the sesame oil, 1 teaspoon of the soy sauce, a pinch of pepper, 1½ teaspoons of the minced garlic, ½ teaspoon of the sesame seeds, the chopped scallion, and a pinch of sugar.

6. Sauté the royal fern with ½ teaspoon of the grapeseed oil, 2¼ teaspoons of the soy sauce, ¾ teaspoon of the sugar, ½ teaspoon of the garlic, and a pinch of pepper over medium-low heat for about 20 minutes, until the fern softens slightly and the ingredients are combined. Set aside.

7. Sauté the shiitake mushrooms with 1 tablespoon of the grapeseed oil and a pinch of the salt over medium heat until soft and golden, 5 minutes. Set aside.

8. Sauté the carrots with 1 tablespoon of the grapeseed oil over medium heat until soft, 8 minutes. Set aside.

9. Sauté the marinated beef with 2 teaspoons of the grapeseed oil over medium-high heat until cooked through, about 5 minutes. Set aside.

10. Mix the gochujang with 2¼ teaspoons of the sesame oil and 2¼ teaspoons of the sugar. Set aside.

11. To serve, scoop rice into individual bowls. Arrange the rest of the ingredients on top of the rice, making small piles of each.

12. In a small nonstick sauté pan, cook a sunny-side-up egg and place on top. Serve the gochujang sauce on the side for each person to mix in their desired amount.

Soon's Bulgogi

(GRILLED RIBEYE)

serves 4 TO 6 | PREP 10 MINUTES PLUS 1 HOUR MARINATING | TOTAL 1 HOUR AND 20 MINUTES

ALL OVER THE United States these days, you can find restaurants promoting authentic Korean BBQ. If you love it and want to make it at home, these Bulgogi and Galbi (page 128) recipes are truly delicious—each packs a flavor punch in their marinades. Soon's daughter Gabrielle told me she loved eating them as a child because they had a tabletop grill for dinner time, and who doesn't like a little flame-grilled meat tableside?

FOR THE BULGOGI

⅓ cup (80 ml) soy sauce

6 tablespoons (85 g) sugar

¼ cup (60 ml) mirin

2 tablespoons sesame oil

2 tablespoons crushed roasted sesame seeds

1 teaspoon freshly ground black pepper

2 tablespoons minced garlic

1 cup (55 g) minced scallions

2 pounds (907 g) thinly sliced ribeye

FOR SERVING

Perilla leaves and/or green leaf lettuce

Ssamjang Sauce (page 129)

Minced garlic

Green chili peppers

Cooked white rice

Kimchi

1. **Prepare the bulgogi.** Combine all of the ingredients except the beef in a large bowl until the sugar dissolves. Carefully add the sliced beef in single layers by hand, as to not tear the meat and to ensure that each piece is coated with the marinade completely. Refrigerate for at least 1 hour.

2. Heat a grill pan over high heat and cook the strips of beef for 1 to 2 minutes.

3. Flip the meat and cook until fully cooked, 1 to 2 more minutes.

4. To serve, set out the meat and all of the ingredients in separate bowls. Place a piece of meat on a perilla leaf and/or a lettuce leaf and top with some ssamjamg sauce, garlic, and green chili pepper. Fold it up to enclose the filling.

5. Serve with rice and kimchi on the side.

Soon's Galbi
(GRILLED BEEF SHORT RIBS)

serves 4 TO 6 | *PREP* 10 MINUTES PLUS 1 HOUR MARINATING | *TOTAL* 1 HOUR AND 20 MINUTES

GALBI ARE THINLY sliced short ribs that are marinated and grilled in a similar fashion to the Bulgogi (page 126), and the two preparations are often served alongside each other.

FOR THE GALBI
2 pounds (910 g) LA-style cut beef short ribs (see Note)

½ cup (120 ml) soy sauce

6 tablespoons (75 g) sugar

¼ cup (60 ml) mirin

2 tablespoons sesame oil

2 tablespoons crushed roasted sesame seeds

1 teaspoon freshly ground black pepper

2 tablespoons minced garlic

1 cup (55 g) minced scallions

FOR SERVING
Perilla leaves and/or green leaf lettuce

Ssamjang Sauce (page 129)

Minced garlic

Green chili peppers

Cooked white rice

Kimchi

1. Rinse the short ribs in fresh cold water and drain excess water.

2. Combine the soy sauce, sugar, mirin, sesame oil, sesame seeds, pepper, garlic, and scallions in a large bowl and mix until the sugar dissolves. Carefully add the meat in single layers by hand, as to not tear the meat and to ensure that each piece is coated with the marinade completely. Refrigerate for a few hours, or better, overnight.

3. Heat a grill pan over high heat and cook the ribs for 1 to 2 minutes.

4. Flip the meat and cook until fully cooked, 1 to 2 more minutes.

5. Remove the meat to a serving plate and cut each piece into bite-sized pieces with scissors.

6. To serve, set out the meat and all of the ingredients in separate bowls. Place a piece of meat on a perilla leaf and/or a lettuce leaf and top with some ssamjamg sauce, garlic, and green chili pepper. Fold it up to enclose the filling.

7. Serve with rice and kimchi on the side.

Note

For this recipe, Soon uses LA-style cut beef short ribs. These ribs are cut across the bone thinly, so each piece is a long, thin strip with 3 horizontal cross-sections of bone along one side. You can purchase short ribs cut this way at a Korean grocery store, or ask your butcher to cut the meat ⅛- to ¼-inch (3- to 6-mm) thick. It's worth the extra step because it allows the meat to absorb the delicious sauce and cook up very quickly!

Soon's college senior
portrait, 1973.

Soon, with her son, Timothy,
in the summer of 1980.

SSAMJANG SAUCE

MAKES APPROXIMATELY ¼ TO ½ CUP (60 TO 120 ML)

¼ cup (60 ml) fermented soybean paste
1 tablespoon minced garlic
1 tablespoon chopped scallion
½ tablespoon sugar
1 tablespoon sesame oil
½ tablespoon crushed roasted sesame seeds
½ teaspoon freshly ground black pepper
1 teaspoon gochujang (spicy red pepper paste)

Combine all of the ingredients in a small bowl. Store in the refrigerator. When ready to serve, Soon suggests adding a teaspoon of water if the mixture is too thick to drizzle on the meat.

◆

Soon's Japchae

(GLASS NOODLE STIR-FRY)

serves — 8 | **PREP** 45 MINUTES | **TOTAL** 1 HOUR AND 15 MINUTES

THIS DELICIOUS NOODLE dish is often made for celebrations because it is both a bit labor intensive and feeds a large group. Traditionally, sweet potato noodles are used, but any starch-based glass noodles can be substituted. As with Bibimbap (page 123), cooking each ingredient separately will enhance the individual flavors, textures, and colors.

1 cup (35 g) dried black fungus mushrooms (5 to 10 mushrooms)

½ pound (227 g) beef tenderloin, thinly sliced

¼ cup (60 ml) sesame oil

Freshly ground black pepper

2 tablespoons minced garlic

½ cup (120 ml), plus 2⅓ tablespoons soy sauce

¼ cup (60 ml), plus 1 teaspoon grapeseed oil

1 pound (455 g) fresh shiitake mushrooms, sliced

Coarse salt

2½ teaspoons sugar

1 large onion, sliced into matchstick-sized sticks

3 medium carrots (about ½ pound/ 227 g), julienned and lightly salted

1 bunch (½ pound/ 227 g) Korean spinach (or regular spinach)

12 ounces (340 g) Korean sweet potato starch noodles or other starch-based glass noodles

1 tablespoon corn syrup

6 scallions, cut into 2-inch (5-cm) pieces

1. Add the black fungus mushrooms to a small pot with enough water to cover, and boil for 1 hour. Drain, remove the base from each, and chop the tops into coarse 1-inch (2.5-cm) pieces. Can be done the night before.

2. Combine the beef, 2 tablespoons of the sesame oil, ¼ teaspoon pepper, 1 tablespoon of the minced garlic, and ¼ cup of the soy sauce in a medium bowl or plastic storage bag. Refrigerate while preparing the rest of the ingredients. Can be made ahead, up to the night before.

3. Heat 1 tablespoon of the grapeseed oil in a large sauté pan over medium-high heat, and cook the shiitake mushrooms with ¼ teaspoon salt until soft and golden, 4 to 5 minutes. Set aside.

4. Add 1 tablespoon of the grapeseed oil to the pan and cook the black fungus mushrooms with ½ teaspoon of the soy sauce and 1 teaspoon of the sugar for 5 minutes. Set aside.

5. Add 1 tablespoon of the grapeseed oil to the pan and cook the onion with a pinch of salt until lightly softened, about 8 minutes. Set aside.

6. Add 1 tablespoon of the grapeseed oil to the pan and cook the carrots with a pinch of salt until lightly softened, about 8 minutes. Set aside.

SOON SUN KANG HUH

7. Add the beef to the pan with its marinade and cook until brown throughout, 3 to 5 minutes. Remove the beef from the sauce and set aside.

8. Meanwhile, bring a large pot filled halfway with water to a boil and prepare an ice water bath. In small batches, dunk the spinach in the boiling water for 30 seconds (5 to 10 seconds if using baby spinach), then shock in the ice water bath and gently squeeze out excess water. Reserve the water in the pot.

9. Heat 1 teaspoon grapeseed oil in the pan over high heat, and add the spinach and 1 teaspoon salt. Sauté for 2 minutes and set aside.

10. Bring the water back to a boil. Add the noodles, cover with a lid, then turn off the heat and let the noodles cook for 10 minutes. Drain, rinse with cold water, and then drain again. Cut the noodles into thirds and set aside.

11. Add the cooked noodles to the same pan with the remaining marinade along with the remaining 6 tablespoons (90 ml) soy sauce, the remaining tablespoon minced garlic, and the corn syrup. Cook until the noodles are warmed and the liquid is slightly reduced, about 5 minutes.

12. Reduce the heat to medium-low and add 1½ teaspoons of the sugar and the remaining 2 tablespoons sesame oil. Toss well and add the shiitake mushrooms, beef, carrots, spinach, black fungus mushrooms, onion, and sliced scallions. Toss again to coat and serve immediately.

A handwritten recipe book Soon brought with her from Korea.

Asia
Niigata, Japan

CHIZUKO IWATA OTTON

◆

CHIZUKO WAS BORN ON A rice farm in Ikegahara, a small village in the city of Ojiya, where rice cultivation thrives due to the heavy snowfall. The Iwatas harvested koshihikari rice, which Chizuko proudly proclaims is still considered the best rice in Japan. Chizuko assisted her parents with their rice production business from a very young age. In addition to tending the rice fields, her father was a sake salesman.

After marrying her American husband, Stephen, Chizuko relocated to New Orleans and had two children, Miyuki and Christopher. She worked at a Japanese restaurant while studying English through textbooks and videos.

Today, she lives in Florida but visits her children often. Her daughter Miyuki, a Culinary Institute of America graduate, runs her own restaurant, named Miyuki, where she serves many Japanese-inspired dishes. Miyuki explained that even after her classical training, when it came time to open up her restaurant, she was drawn to her roots. Her mother's food inspires all of her dishes, and she loves when Chizuko comes to the restaurant to help her prep and come up with new menu items.

Chizuko's Sesame String Beans

serves 6 TO 8 AS A SIDE DISH | PREP 10 MINUTES
TOTAL 15 MINUTES

1 pound (455 g) string beans

5 tablespoons toasted sesame seeds, ground with a mortar and pestle

½ teaspoon granulated sugar

1 tablespoon mirin

2 teaspoons soy sauce

1. Blanch the string beans in hot boiling water until crisp-tender, 2 to 4 minutes, then shock in an ice bath.

2. Toss with the remaining ingredients and serve at room temperature.

Chizuko's Cucumber Salad

serves 6 TO 8 AS A SIDE DISH | PREP 5 MINUTES
TOTAL 10 MINUTES

½ large English cucumber

1 teaspoon coarse salt

2 teaspoons Wakame seaweed

1 small stick (1 to 2 ounces/28 to 55 g) imitation crab

7 teaspoons ponzu

5 teaspoons soy sauce

1 tablespoon mirin

1 to 2 pieces sliced ginger (optional, to taste)

1. Slice the cucumber into very thin rounds and place in a shallow dish. Add the salt and let sit for a few minutes.

2. Drain the cucumber, then gently squeeze it to remove excess water.

3. Soak the seaweed in a bowl of room-temperature water for 5 minutes. Drain and set aside.

4. Shred the imitation crab into small pieces by gently peeling off pieces.

5. Combine the cucumber, seaweed, and crab in a small bowl.

6. Combine the ponzu, soy sauce, and mirin in a separate bowl, then pour over the cucumber mixture.

7. Serve with the ginger on top, if desired.

Chizuko's Yosenabe

(SEAFOOD AND VEGETABLE HOT POT)

serves 6 TO 8, DEPENDING ON AMOUNT OF INGREDIENTS ADDED TO THE BROTH | *PREP* 40 MINUTES | *TOTAL* 45 TO 50 MINUTES

YOSENABE IS A delicious Japanese hot-pot meal. It is comprised of a soup stock in which all of the additional ingredients are cooked. Chizuko explained that traditionally, you cook the hot broth in a *donabe* (a large, covered bowl), and guests partake from this communal dish. Don't forget to serve with sake! She often serves her Sesame String Beans (page 133) and Cucumber Salad (page 133) alongside the yosenabe.

FOR THE BROTH
8 pieces kelp

1 cup (25 g) bonito flakes

1½ teaspoons coarse salt

2 tablespoons sake (Chizuko prefers Gekkeikan)

2 tablespoons mirin

1 tablespoon soy sauce

FOR THE YOSENABE
2 carrots, cut into large squares

½ Napa cabbage, cut into large squares

½ leek, washed well and cut into large squares

8 ounces (227 g) oyster mushrooms

8 ounces (227 g) firm tofu, cut into large squares

8 ounces (227 g) Chilean sea bass or salmon

8 ounces (227 g) large shrimp, deveined, shell removed

8 ounces (227 g) scallops

8 ounces (227 g) clams

1. **Make the broth.** Wipe the kelp with a tea towel, then make thin score lines along its sides with a small knife.

2. Combine the kelp with 8 cups (2 L) water in a large stockpot. Leave to soak for 30 minutes.

3. Bring the pot to a simmer over medium heat. The moment it comes to a simmer, remove the kelp and discard (the kelp is used for flavoring only).

4. Add the bonito flakes, bring the water to a boil, and cook for 3 minutes. Strain the flakes out of the broth, discard the flakes, and reduce the heat to a simmer.

5. Add the salt, sake, mirin, and soy sauce and bring the broth back up to a simmer.

6. ***Make the yosenabe.*** Each ingredient should be added to the broth pot based on its cooking time. The vegetables take the longest to cook, so they are added first: Simmer the carrots, cabbage, leek, and mushrooms, uncovered, for 2 to 3 minutes. Then add the tofu and simmer for 4 to 5 more minutes. Finally, add the seafood and cook, covered, until the shrimp and scallops are cooked through and the clams have opened, 5 to 6 more minutes.

7. Uncover and skim the foam from the top of the broth.

8. If you did not cook in a donabe, which can be transferred to the table for serving, remove all the items separately and transfer the broth to a very large serving bowl.

9. Add each item to the bowl, careful to place all like items together. Guests can then serve themselves from this communal pot.

CHIZUKO IWATA OTTON

135

MAGDALENA "MAGDA" RAMOS SHADER

◆

MAGDA RAMOS SHADER DOESN'T PLAN on living the rest of her life in the United States—a large portion of her big, loving family anxiously awaits her return to the Philippines when her husband retires. But for now, she happily works to help raise her American great-nieces and -nephews.

While Magda is not a grandmother biologically, if you ask any of her nieces or nephews, she is an honorary grandmother to all of them. Why? Because whenever someone needs something, Auntie Magda's only response is "yes." It doesn't matter if she is busy or maybe feeling a little bit under the weather—when her phone rings, she is always ready to lend a helping hand.

At all family occasions, Magda can be found behind the stove, expertly flipping the lumpia (page 137) in the hot oil, and carefully watching her pork adobo (page 139) boil, because no family get-together would be complete without these two most-requested of her many delicious dishes. If she can't make it to a birthday celebration, she still makes noodles, to ensure a long life, and eats them herself, sending love and well wishes from her home in Jersey City, New Jersey, all the way to the Philippines, Connecticut, or wherever else, because that is just what Auntie Magda always remembers to do.

When asked about her life's successes, she immediately references her nieces and nephews back in the Philippines. Quietly and humbly, over her years working in the United States, Magda has sent what little money she has earned back home to assist with their college tuition. Now, as her "children" are grown with thriving careers, she is elated about their accomplishments. She doesn't have much in the way of material things, but the pride she feels for her family is, for her, her biggest achievement.

Magda's Lumpia
(FRIED PORK SPRING ROLLS)

makes 6 DOZEN | *PREP* 15 MINUTES | *TOTAL* 40 MINUTES

YOU WOULD BE hard-pressed to find someone that couldn't eat ten or twenty of these crispy little pork spring rolls in a sitting. Magda uses premade spring roll sheets for hers, but she cuts them into thirds to make mini rolls. Her niece, Maria, loves serving them with Thai chili sauce, but not Magda: She eats them with the traditional vinegar and garlic dip. Either way, they are delicious and *highly* addictive—I dare you to eat just one!

FOR THE ROLLS

1 medium carrot, cut into quarters

6 garlic cloves

1 medium white onion, cut into quarters

1 pound (455 g) ground pork

1 teaspoon coarse salt

1 teaspoon freshly ground black pepper

1 teaspoon MSG (optional)

1 package (8-inch/20-cm square) spring roll pastry sheets (Magda prefers Spring Home TYJ Spring Roll Pastry)

1 large egg

1 teaspoon all-purpose flour

3 to 4 cups (720 to 960 ml) vegetable oil

FOR THE DIPPING SAUCE

1 cup (240 ml) white vinegar

1 teaspoon freshly ground black pepper

1 garlic clove, minced

1. ***Make the rolls.*** Chop the carrot, garlic, and onion in a food processor until finely minced but not yet a paste.

2. Combine the vegetables with the pork, salt, pepper, and MSG (if using) in a large bowl.

3. Place all of the pastry sheets on a cutting board and fold letter style into thirds. Cut the pile into thirds across the folds.

4. Beat the egg with the flour and 1 tablespoon water in a small bowl. Set up an assembly line of egg mixture, wrappers, and pork mixture.

5. Place a strip of pastry on a flat surface with the short end facing you. Place a heaping teaspoon of filling on the end closest to you.

6. Leaving the sides open, tightly and evenly roll up the lumpia, keeping the far end taut so the ends remain even and tight. Once you reach the far end, seal the wrapper with a swipe of the egg mixture along the edge. Repeat until all of the filling is used.

7. Meanwhile, heat the oil in a large pot to 350°F (175°C). Add 5 to 6 lumpia at a time and cook until the wrappers become golden brown and the filling is very dark on the ends, 4 to 5 minutes.

8. Drain on paper towels. Repeat for the remaining lumpia.

9. ***Make the dipping sauce.*** Combine the vinegar, pepper, and garlic in a small bowl.

MAGDALENA RAMOS SHADER

137

ASIA | *Bauan, Philippines*

Magda's Pork Adobo

serves 6 AS A MAIN DISH, 10 AS AN APPETIZER | PREP 10 MINUTES | TOTAL 1 HOUR AND 20 MINUTES, PLUS 48 HOURS

TRADITIONALLY, FILIPINO ADOBO, the unofficial national dish, is made with chicken thighs or pork belly. However, Magda loves to make her version of this dish with pork ribs, asking her butcher to slice the racks in half horizontally to create little riblets. Not only are they finger-licking good to eat on their own, serving them over rice to sop up the fantastic sauce is even better.

According to Magda, adobo intensity is a matter of taste that varies from home to home and region to region. The ratios in her recipe create a balanced sauce, but you can adjust the vinegar and sweet soy sauce until it is just as tart or sweet as you like.

2 pounds (907 g) pork rib racks, cut in half horizontally (see Note)

2 bay leaves

8 garlic cloves, peeled

½ medium onion, sliced

½ cup (120 ml) high-quality soy sauce (Magda prefers Silver Swan)

¼ cup (60 ml) sweet soy sauce (Magda prefers ABC Dark Sweet Soy Sauce)

1 teaspoon coarse salt

1 teaspoon freshly ground black pepper

½ cup (120 ml) white vinegar

1 small white potato, peeled (optional)

1 cup (190 g) cooked jasmine rice

Continues

MAGDALENA RAMOS SHADER

1. Place the ribs in a large glass casserole dish bone side up. Add the bay leaves, garlic, and onion.

2. Combine both soy sauces, salt, pepper, and vinegar in a medium mixing bowl.

3. Pour the marinade over the ribs and mix to coat. Marinate the ribs for 2 days, covered, in the refrigerator.

4. Place the ribs and all of the marinade in a large stock pot and heat over high heat until the marinade begins to bubble. Lower the heat to a simmer and cover.

5. Simmer the ribs for 1 hour, until they are cooked through and the meat is tender. Magda's tip: If you taste the sauce while you are cooking and find it to be too tart, drop in a small, whole peeled potato at the 30-minute mark. This will mellow out the sauce, and the potato itself will taste quite good when you fish it out!

6. Remove the lid and bring the heat up to medium-high and cook until the sauce thickens and coats the back of a spoon, about 10 more minutes. Mix to cover the ribs in the sauce. Serve with the rice.

Note

To make a more traditional adobo, substitute 2 pounds (910 g) bone-in skinless chicken thighs for the ribs. The process is the same, but you only have to marinate the meat for one day! Make sure to cut a slit in the flesh near the bone to let all those delicious juices seep in.

LYDIA LOPEZ ZABALA

◆

LYDIA LOPEZ ZABALA WAS RAISED in Malued, a rural area of the Philippines. She grew up in a loving home where her parents pursued many careers to raise their six children. Her father, Eliodoro, was an insurance agent who also owned and managed a few local businesses such as a grocery store and a canteen located in a local theater. Her mother, Lucia, took care of the children and managed the grocery store. Their life was simple but joyful.

No stranger to hard work, Lydia attended the University of Pangasinan. After graduation, she enrolled in the Santa Rita School of Nursing. During this time, she entered the Miss Dagupan beauty pageant at the urging of her friends and family, and won. This win led her to star in two movies, but after a short stint in acting, she decided to follow her real dream: starting a family of her own. She had two children, Edwin and Imelda, but unfortunately her son Edwin passed away when he was just a child.

Because of her adventurous spirit, Lydia decided to immigrate to California with her daughter in 1987. She felt it was an opportunity of a lifetime, and immediately found work as a certified nursing assistant. But as exciting as the United States was, she missed the flavors of home. Without recipes to reference, she began cooking a fusion of Filipino-Chinese food that brought to life the dishes of her homeland infused with flavors found in her new home.

Lydia began to bring her culinary creations to work at the Sonoma Development Center, and everyone was so impressed with her dishes that they encouraged her to open a restaurant. Because she was raised by entrepreneurs, she had the courage to do it. She opened ilang-ilang on Sonoma Boulevard in Vallejo, California, in 2002.

For nearly ten years, Lydia juggled much like her parents did: she continued working as a nurse and looking after her grandchildren all while running her successful restaurant. Her pancit bihon (page 142) was a very popular menu item and she worked hard to perfect it, along with other Filipino dishes such as flan (page 143) and adobo.

Finally, in 2012, she retired and put all of her focus on her greatest love: her family. Although she is enjoying the fruits of her life of hard work full time, she can still be found catering and making Pancit Bihon for family events.

Lydia's Pancit Bihon

(CHICKEN AND VEGETABLE NOODLE STIR-FRY)

serves 8 | PREP 20 MINUTES | TOTAL 40 MINUTES

THIS DISH, ORIGINALLY adapted from the Chinese, is a delicious blend of stir-fried chicken and vegetables folded into pancit (thin rice) noodles. The dish is traditionally made for birthdays: the long noodles, eaten in happy times, ensure a long life for the celebrant. No matter what the occasion, Lydia's daughter, grandchildren, nieces, and nephews ask her to bring it to all the large family get-togethers, as it's delicious and the large batch is great for feeding a crowd.

3 tablespoons vegetable oil

2 garlic cloves, finely chopped

1 medium onion, sliced

1 pound (455 g) chicken breasts, cut into 1-inch (2.5-cm) strips

1 teaspoon sea salt

1 teaspoon freshly ground black pepper

¼ cup (60 ml) soy sauce

2 medium carrots, julienned

½ small cabbage, cut into 1-inch (2.5-cm) strips

2 stalks celery, sliced into ½-inch (2.5-cm) pieces

1 chicken bouillon cube

8 ounces (227 g) thin rice (pancit) noodles

1. Heat 2 tablespoons of the vegetable oil in a large frying pan over high heat. Add the garlic, onion, and chicken and cook, stirring, until the onion has softened and the chicken is no longer pink, about 3 minutes. Season with the salt and pepper. Add 2 tablespoons of the soy sauce and stir to combine.

2. Add the carrots, cover the pan, and cook for 3 minutes, until the carrots begin to soften.

3. Add the cabbage and celery and cook, stirring, until the cabbage wilts, about 3 minutes, then remove the mixture to a bowl and set aside. Do not rinse the pan.

4. Add 3 cups (720 ml) water, the bouillon cube, and the remaining 2 tablespoons soy sauce to the pan. Bring to a boil.

5. Rinse the noodles and add them to the pan along with the remaining tablespoon of oil. Gently stir to distribute the noodles, then lower the heat to a simmer, cover, and cook until the noodles are soft and the liquid has fully absorbed, about 6 minutes, stirring occasionally to prevent the noodles from sticking.

6. Return the vegetables and chicken to the pan and cook, stirring, for 2 more minutes, until heated through. Adjust seasoning to taste before serving.

Lydia's Flan

serves 8 | **PREP** 15 MINUTES | **TOTAL** 1 HOUR AND 15 MINUTES

THIS DECADENT AND sweet custardy dessert is a favorite for Lydia's family. With only five ingredients, it comes together very quickly.

1 cup (200 g) sugar

6 large eggs

1 (14-ounce/397-g) can sweetened condensed milk

1 (12-ounce/340 g) can evaporated milk

1 teaspoon vanilla extract

1. Preheat oven to 325°F (165°C). Place an 11-inch, 1½-quart (1.4 L) baking dish inside a larger baking pan with sides that are taller than your baking dish (a large disposable aluminum pan can be used). Set aside.

2. Heat the sugar and 3 tablespoons water in a small saucepan over medium-high heat. Let it come to a boil. When the liquid begins to turn color, gently swirl the pan until the sugar turns a dark golden amber, about 8 minutes. Pour the sugar into the bottom of the smaller baking dish.

3. Beat the eggs in a large bowl until combined. Stir in the condensed milk, then the evaporated milk and vanilla extract. (Lydia often uses a blender for this step.)

4. Pour the mixture over the caramelized sugar in the baking dish.

5. Place the larger baking pan into the oven and pour boiling water into it until it comes halfway up the sides of the smaller pan. This water bath cooks the flan more gently.

6. Bake for about 1 hour, until the top of the flan turns a light-yellow color and is firm but not stiff. Remove and let cool slightly, approximately 10 minutes.

7. Use an offset spatula to loosen the edges of the flan. Place a serving plate atop the pan and flip the pan over to release the flan. (Or, leave it as is!) The flan can be served warm or at room temperature.

A photo from Lydia's acting portfolio from 1963. Her screen name was Susan Ledesma.

LYDIA LOPEZ ZABALA

KHURSHID "KAY" YEZDI MEHTA

Khurshid, also known as Kay,

REMEMBERS HER CHILDHOOD IN MUMBAI as a happy one, filled with close friends and a strong, diverse community. As a child, many of her companions were of Indian heritage like her, but they did not share the same religious beliefs. In this small group, the dietary practices of each family were dictated by belief rather than geographical location. This allowed many different indigenous cuisines to share a block, town, or, in Kay's instance, a multi-apartment building.

As a child, she and this eclectic group of friends used these differences to their advantage. After hours of playing, instead of each child heading to their respective home for dinner, the children would hop from door to door, investigating the ingredients on each countertop to ascertain the evening meal that each mother was preparing before making a decision about where to eat. Depending on the mood of the hungry group, the chosen family would set out extra dishes and the dinner would be shared. The hunt for delicious food and friendship always superseded belief differences, giving Kay an appreciation for the cuisines of others from a very young age.

Kay's story of immigration to the United States is also quite impressive. After marrying, her husband Yezdi's career as a petroleum engineer required a transfer to Singapore. After residing there for a little over a decade and having their two sons, Sherazad and Darius, the family immigrated to the United States in the '80s. As a young, motivated mother, she began working at a bank in the service department as a teller. Her husband's tragic and untimely death in 1993 left her to carry on raising her teenage children on her own. However, her hard work and dedication paid off—slowly but surely, she moved up the corporate ladder of the bank. She recently retired as a highly respected vice president.

Today, she spends her time traveling the world and doting on her grandchildren. In addition, she is studying to become a *mobedyar*, a priest's assistant, a position that has been held only by men in India for centuries. She will be the first female mobedyar in New Jersey, and among the first female mobedyars in the world. Her family is extremely proud of this grand accomplishment and are looking forward to her assistance in the sacred Navjote ceremony for her grandchildren to initiate them into the Zoroastrian faith. She will be able to participate in a number of tasks, such as maintaining the fire throughout the ceremony.

An important portion of the ceremony is instilling the important tenets of Zoroastrianism: good thoughts, good words, and good deeds. After cooking with Khurshid and sharing her delicious meal, I would like to add a fourth tenet: good food.

LIKE SUGAR IN MILK

As a proud Parsi woman, Kay's food is rooted in her culture and the Zoroastrian religion. Kay recounted the story of how her ancestors fled religious persecution in Persia (present-day Iran) and, by chance, found their boats washed up on Indian shores in approximately 755 CE. When the Zoroastrians arrived, they requested an important meeting with the ruler, Jadi Rana, for permission to settle. Initially, he was resistant, and presented them with a large pitcher of milk filled to the brim, saying, "The kingdom is full, we cannot accept your people." However, a Zoroastrian priest thought differently. He stirred a spoonful of sugar into the milk, and said, "Please see, the milk will not overflow—instead we will assimilate and make it sweet." Jadi Rana was so taken by the gesture he allowed the immigrants to settle.

Kay's Turkey Kebabs

serves — 4 (MAKES 12 TO 14) | **PREP** 20 MINUTES | **TOTAL** 2 HOURS

KAY SERVES THESE kebabs as a delicious appetizer. Bite-sized, flavor-packed turkey meatballs come together quickly and fry up crispy and juicy in minutes. She suggests serving them with an ice-cold beer and assures me that you will eat more than you are willing to admit.

1 pound (455 g) ground turkey

1 small onion, minced (about ½ cup/65 g)

2 tablespoons Ginger-Garlic Paste (opposite)

½ teaspoon turmeric powder

½ teaspoon chili powder

1 to 2 green chili peppers, finely chopped (optional), seeds removed, also optional depending on heat level

1 tablespoon ground coriander

1 tablespoon ground cumin

1 teaspoon chopped cilantro

1½ slices white bread, soaked in water and squeezed dry

Vegetable oil

½ cup (50 g) plain bread crumbs, optional

Kay and her husband Yezdi on their wedding day, 1971.

KHURSHID YEZDI MEHTA

1. Combine all of the ingredients except the vegetable oil and bread crumbs in a large bowl. Let the mixture sit for 30 minutes for the flavors to develop.

2. Oil your hands with a little vegetable oil, then take about 3 tablespoons of the mixture and roll it into a ball about 2 inches (5 cm) in diameter. Repeat for the remaining mixture.

3. Pour the bread crumbs (if using) in a shallow dish and lightly roll each kebab in the crumbs to coat. (This makes for a crispy coating; sometimes Kay prefers the kebabs smooth and skips this step.)

4. Heat about ½ inch (12 mm) of vegetable oil in a large cast iron skillet to 350°F (175°C). Gently add the kebabs in batches and fry, without crowding the pan, rolling them so that each side is browned, about 10 to 12 minutes total. They should be lightly browned on the outside with no pink on the inside.

5. Transfer to paper towels to drain. Serve hot. Kebabs can be frozen for up to a month after frying.

KAY'S GINGER-GARLIC PASTE

MAKES ⅓ CUP (80 ML)

Kay uses this mixture frequently, so she makes quite a lot all at once, using a pound each of the garlic and ginger. If you choose to make a similarly large quantity, add 1 teaspoon table salt so it will keep longer in the fridge. Alternatively, you can freeze it for up to a month for future use.

½-inch (12-mm) piece ginger root, peeled

1 head garlic, cloves peeled

Soak the ginger and garlic for 1 hour in enough water to cover.

Drain and grind to a paste in a food processor with 1 to 2 teaspoons water.

The idea of a single blend called *curry powder* is actually a British tradition. In India, each woman creates her own blend of spices; her own "curry." Some prefer more cumin or others might add extra coriander. For Kay, the most important ingredient in her curry blend is this paste.

Kay's Crab Curry

serves 8 | **PREP** 15 MINUTES | **TOTAL** 50 MINUTES

THIS IS THE recipe Kay was most excited to teach me. It just so happens that Kay and her family lived next door to my husband's childhood home, and Phil (known as P.J. when he was a child) and Kay's son Darius were inseparable best friends, so much so that she lovingly refers to my husband as "P.J. Mehta." She loved making this dish and watching Phil, a native Long Island boy, slurp it down with her sons.

3 tablespoons vegetable or corn oil

⅓ cup (80 ml) Ginger-Garlic Paste (page 147)

¼ cup (25 g) finely desiccated or powdered coconut

½ teaspoon turmeric powder

3 tablespoons coriander seeds, roasted and ground to a powder

1 tablespoon cumin seeds, roasted and ground to a powder

1 tablespoon chili powder

2 cups (480 ml) tomato juice

8 to 10 curry leaves

4 small, dry red chilis, whole, Indian, or Szechuan

1 teaspoon coarse salt, or more to taste

1-inch (2.5-cm) block tamarind, soaked in 2 cups (480 ml) hot water until soft enough to squeeze the pulp out of the middle

3 pounds (1.4 kg) fresh blue crab or shrimp

2 cups (360 g) cooked white basmati rice (Kay prefers Zebra)

1. Heat the oil in a deep pan over medium heat. Add the ginger-garlic paste and cook, stirring, until the water evaporates, about 2 minutes. Add the coconut, turmeric, coriander, cumin, and chili powder. Stir to combine and cook for another minute. Be careful not to let the mixture brown, or it will become bitter.

2. Add the tomato juice, curry leaves, red chilis, and salt. Add 1 teaspoon of the tamarind pulp, or more to taste. (The more pulp, the more sour the final curry will be.) Stir to combine.

3. Bring to a boil, then reduce to a simmer and cook for 10 minutes. If using shrimp, add to the pot, cover, and simmer until the shrimp is no longer pink, 5 minutes. If using crab, add to the pot, cover, and simmer until completely cooked through, 20 minutes.

4. Serve over steamed rice.

↖ The sace is a metallic tray that holds the ceremonial utensils used in important Zoroastrian ceremonies like Navjote.

KHURSHID YEZDI MEHTA

Kay's Ravo
(SEMOLINA PUDDING)

serves 4 TO 6 | *PREP* 10 MINUTES | *TOTAL* 15 MINUTES

PARSIS MAKE THIS delicious, creamy semolina pudding, called *ravo*, to celebrate holidays and birthdays. (Darius, Kay's son, confirmed he ate it on every birthday as a child.) Traditionally, the leftover ravo is heated up in the morning with a little more milk for a decadent breakfast, an "after party," if you will. My favorite part is the butter-poached toasted almonds and raisins—it's the perfect sweet and crunchy topping to the milky, buttery farina.

6 tablespoons (85 g) unsalted butter

2 tablespoons blanched, slivered almonds, plus more for serving

1 cup (145 g) raisins, plus more for serving

½ cup (90 g) sooji or farina (fine semolina flour)

3 cups (720 ml) whole milk

2 tablespoons white sugar

1 large egg, beaten

1 to 2 tablespoons vanilla extract, to taste

2 pinches coarse salt

Ground nutmeg, to taste (optional)

1. Heat 3 tablespoons of the butter in a small pan over low heat. When it begins to bubble, add the almonds and stir continuously until they turn golden brown, about 3 minutes. Transfer to paper towels to drain. Return the pan to the heat without cleaning it.

2. Add the raisins to the pan and stir to coat. Cook until plump, about 2 minutes. Transfer to the paper towels with the almonds.

3. Heat the remaining 3 tablespoons butter in a clean saucepan over medium heat. Add the sooji and cook, stirring, until the grains are well coated and all the butter has been absorbed, about 1 minute.

4. Remove from the heat and slowly add the milk and sugar, stirring continuously until smooth. Return the pan to the stove over medium heat and cook, stirring, until the mixture begins to bubble, about 2 minutes. Immediately remove from the heat and let cool for 5 minutes.

5. Add the beaten egg to the mixture in a steady stream while stirring, so it doesn't curdle. Once all the egg is incorporated, add the vanilla and the salt.

6. Taste your ravo at this point. If you prefer a thicker consistency, it is ready to serve. If you prefer a thinner consistency, add a bit more milk.

7. Pour into a serving bowl and garnish with the almonds and raisins and a sprinkle of nutmeg (if using).

Note

You can use cranberries and/or chopped crystalized cherries instead of raisins if you prefer a more tart topping. If you have leftovers and the mixture thickens overnight, add more milk when reheating. It can be eaten warm for breakfast or cold as a dessert.

KHURSHID YEZDI MEHTA

SHOBHANA KANAKIA

SHOBHANA KANAKIA KNEW HER HUSBAND, Mahendra, for only thirteen days before their arranged marriage, and they immigrated to the United States shortly after their wedding. Forty years and three grown children—Meera, Amy, and Vijay—later, it looks like it turned out to be a lovely arrangement!

When she first moved to the United States for the chance at a better life, Shobhana immediately began looking for work. She loved children, so she took small jobs babysitting, eventually opening a small daycare center that she ran out of her home in addition to working other odd jobs to help her family prosper.

When she wasn't working, Shobhana also began to learn to cook "American" dishes. Her young children shied away from the traditional Indian cuisine she knew how to make, so she learned how to cook items they would eat willingly while still cooking the food of her homeland for her husband.

Shobhana's daughter Meera was once embarrassed by how different Indian cuisine was from the food of her American friends, but now these are the foods she craves when she returns to her parents' home to visit. They are the foods she associates with her family, her upbringing, and her happy childhood. As a new mom herself, she appreciates how Shobhana always put the family first, and she marvels at the time her mother put into learning and preparing new dishes to keep her children healthy and well fed.

Shobhana's Lentil Dal

serves 6 TO 8 | PREP 15 MINUTES | TOTAL 45 MINUTES

THIS SIMPLE VEGETARIAN dal made with brown lentils is easy to put together. It is nutritious, and depending on your heat tolerance, can be made spicier by simply increasing the amount of chili powder to taste. Dals can be made with red or yellow lentils, too; adjust the cooking time based on the package directions. Shobhana likes to serve her dal over steaming basmati or jasmine rice.

1 cup (190 g) brown lentils

3 tablespoons vegetable oil

1 small onion, minced

2 garlic cloves, thinly sliced

1 teaspoon turmeric powder

1 teaspoon ground coriander

1 teaspoon ground cumin

Pinch of red chili powder

2 teaspoons salt

1 tomato, chopped

1 cup (40 g) chopped cilantro

Cooked jasmine or basmati rice

1. Combine the lentils and 4 cups (960 ml) water in a large pot and bring to a boil. Cook the lentils for 10 minutes to soften. Transfer the lentils with the cooking water to a bowl and set aside.

2. Clean the pot, add the oil, and heat over medium heat. Add the onion and garlic and cook until lightly browned, about 8 minutes.

3. Add the turmeric, coriander, cumin, chili powder, and salt and stir to combine. Return the lentils with cooking water to the pan, bring to a boil, and add the tomato. Cook for 10 minutes.

4. Stir in the cilantro just before serving, and serve over white rice.

Shobhana's Dosas

serves 6 (MAKES 12) | **PREP** 15 MINUTES | **TOTAL** 17 HOURS, PLUS OVERNIGHT

SHOBHANA LOVES MAKING dosas when her children visit. Now as adults, they love and appreciate the thin pancakes she makes by the dozen and serves with her homemade delicious toppings and fillings. Dosas can be served many different ways, either with a filling like Aloo Sabzi (page 156), topped with a condiment like Coconut Chutney (page 157), or with ingredients like peppers and onions simply stirred into the batter.

½ cup (96 g) urad dal (split lentil beans)

1 cup (185 g) long-grain white rice

¾ teaspoon coarse salt

¾ teaspoon ground cumin

½ cup (120 ml) vegetable oil

1. Rinse and drain the urad dal, then place it in a bowl with 2 cups (480 ml) water. Rise and drain the rice, then place it in a bowl with 3 cups (720 ml) water. Soak for at least 8 hours, then drain both.

2. Puree the soaked urad dal with ¼ cup (60 ml) water in a blender, then set aside.

3. Rinse the blender. Puree the soaked rice with ½ cup (120 ml) water in the blender. Return the urad dal to the blender with the rice mixture and add 2 cups (480 ml) cold water. Blend until smooth.

4. Add the salt and cumin and blend to combine. Let the batter rest overnight, covered in the refrigerator.

5. Remove the batter from the refrigerator and let sit on the counter for 8 hours in a covered bowl to soften the ingredients.

6. Heat 1 teaspoon of the vegetable oil in an 8- or 9-inch (20- or 23-cm) cast-iron crepe pan over medium-high heat. Ladle about ½ cup (120 ml) of the batter into the pan and spread into a thin layer. Drizzle a few drops of oil around the edges and over the middle and cook for four to five minutes. Lift one edge with a spatula to check the color; it's ready when it is golden brown.

7. Remove the dosa from the pan and add a few heaping spoonfuls of Aloo Sabzi (page 156) to the middle and fold the left and right edges in to the center.

8. Serve with Coconut Chutney (page 157) drizzled on top.

Shobhana's Aloo Sabzi

serves 4 | **PREP** 15 MINUTES | **TOTAL** 45 MINUTES

THIS DELICIOUS POTATO dish is a traditional filling for dosas, but is also great on its own. The turmeric gives it a beautiful yellow hue and the mustard seeds and ginger pack a flavor punch.

1 large Idaho potato (about 1 pound/455 g), peeled and cut into 1-inch (2.5-cm) pieces

1 tablespoon vegetable oil

1 teaspoon brown mustard seeds

½ teaspoon urad dal (spicy lentil beans)

1 large yellow onion, cut into 1-inch (2.5-cm) pieces

1 teaspoon minced fresh ginger

1 teaspoon minced green chili (seeds optional)

Coarse salt

1 teaspoon turmeric powder

1 teaspoon cilantro, chopped

1. Place the potato in a pot with enough water to cover. Bring to a boil and cook until fork-tender, about 10 minutes. Drain and set aside.

2. Heat the vegetable oil in a large sauté pan over medium heat and add the mustard seeds and urad dal. Toast the seeds until the oil becomes fragrant, 1 to 2 minutes. Add the onion, ginger, and chili and cook until the onion softens and becomes translucent, about 8 minutes.

3. Add the potato to the pan, sprinkle ½ teaspoon salt and the turmeric all over and cook, stirring, to heat the potato through, about 3 minutes.

4. Remove from the heat, add the cilantro, and season to taste with additional salt.

5. Serve as a side or use as a filling for Shobhana's Dosas (page 154).

Shobhana's Coconut Chutney

makes 2½ CUPS (600 ML) | PREP 10 MINUTES | TOTAL 25 MINUTES

2 ounces ginger, peeled and cut into chunks

1 ¼-ounce small, thin green chili pepper, such as a serrano, stem removed (seeds optional)

1½ cups (150 g) freshly grated coconut

½ cup (90 g) dried split chickpeas

¾ cup (180 ml) whole milk yogurt

1 tablespoon coarse salt

1 tablespoon vegetable oil

½ teaspoon brown or black mustard seeds

5 Indian bay leaves

1. Grind the ginger and pepper in a blender until fine. Add the coconut, chickpeas, and 1 cup (240 ml) water. Puree until combined, about 2 minutes. You can add more water, a little at a time, if the mixture is not blending well.

2. Add the yogurt and salt and blend until smooth, another 3 minutes. Pour the mixture into a bowl and set aside.

3. Heat the oil in a medium sauté pan over medium heat. When the oil begins to shimmer, add the mustard seeds and cook until they pop, about 2 minutes.

4. Add the bay leaves. They should begin to crackle and brown. Shake the pan for about 10 seconds and then pour the oil on top of the chutney. Stir to combine.

5. Serve as a garnish for Shobhana's Dosas (page 154).

"It's the hand that cooks the dish."

—NIKKI THÉODORE

CENTRAL & SOUTH AMERICA

Minas Gerais, Brazil

MORGANA OLIVEIRA SOARES SPILLER

◆

HOME, TO MORGANA, IS HER grandmother, Maura, preparing a delicious meal at the stove in Brazil. While her mother, Rosa, tended to Morgana and her brother, Maura would fill their stomachs with traditional Brazilian food every night of the week. Rice and beans always made up the base, and different meat courses rounded out the meal.

Morgana left Brazil as a teenager to attend college. She subsequently married an American, Chris, and eventually made the United States her permanent home. But she returns every year to see all of the family she left behind. Morgana and Chris have made it a priority to maintain Brazilian traditions in their home so that their daughter, Isabella, stays connected to her heritage. Although she is American by birth, Isabella is fluent in Portuguese and, of course, the ins and outs of traditional Brazilian fare.

Morgana's Feijão Tropeiro

(BEANS WITH FRIED BACON AND EGGS)

serves 4 TO 5 | *PREP* 35 MINUTES | *TOTAL* 1 HOUR

ACCORDING TO MORGANA, weekday meals are simple in Brazil, but the weekends are for gathering together and eating big, hearty meals as a family. This dish, which translates to "cattlemen's beans," is named so because these nonperishable ingredients— beans, salted meat, and flour—could be carried and combined easily by *tropeiros*, or cattlemen, during their journeys. This dish is a staple weekend meal in Morgana's home. Her grandmother will usually double or triple this recipe to feed their entire big, extended family.

4 (15½-ounce/445-g) cans red beans, drained

¼ cup (60 ml) vegetable oil

2 yellow plantains, diced

4 ounces (115 g) smoked thick-cut bacon, diced

2 small yellow onions, minced

6 ounces linguiça calabresa (Brazilian sausage), diced

12 ounces (340 g) ground sweet or hot pork sausage, removed from casing and crumbled

2 large eggs

6 garlic cloves, finely chopped

3 scallions, finely chopped

3 tablespoons finely chopped fresh parsley

10 large collard leaves, cut chiffonade

4 large eggs, hard-boiled, 3 finely chopped and 1 thinly sliced

¼ cup (30 g) toasted cassava or yucca flour

1. Heat the vegetable oil in a small sauté pan over medium heat, then add the plantains and cook, stirring, to brown all sides, 3 to 4 minutes. Set aside.

2. Heat a large Dutch oven over medium heat, then add the diced bacon. Slowly cook the bacon until it is fully cooked and crispy, 3 to 5 minutes. Remove the bacon from the pan with a slotted spoon and set aside, reserving the bacon fat.

3. Add the onion to the bacon fat and cook over medium heat until translucent, about 8 minutes.

4. Add both types of sausage to the pot and cook until golden brown, 5 to 7 minutes.

5. Push the mixture to the sides of the pan, creating a well in the middle. Crack the eggs into the middle of the pan and cook until the whites are set.

6. Break the yolks with the side of a wooden spoon and stir to combine with the other ingredients in the pot until fully incorporated.

7. Add the garlic and cook, stirring to soften, 3 minutes, then add the scallions and parsley.

8. Make another well in the middle of the pot and add the collard greens, reserving a handful. Cook the collards in the well until wilted, about 2 minutes, and then stir to combine with the ingredients in the pot.

9. Add the 3 chopped hard-boiled eggs and the beans. Sprinkle the flour over and stir to combine.

10. Add the cooked plantains and cook for 2 more minutes.

11. Serve sprinkled with the reserved collards. Place the sliced hard-boiled egg on top. Serve immediately.

MORGANA OLIVEIRA SOARES SPILLER

CENTRAL & SOUTH AMERICA | *Minas Gerais, Brazil*

Morgana's Brigadeiros

(CHOCOLATE BONBONS)

makes ABOUT 24 (1-INCH/2.5-CM) BONBONS | *PREP* 5 MINUTES | *TOTAL* 1 HOUR AND 15 MINUTES

DELICIOUS CHOCOLATE BONBONS, called *brigadeiros*, are a traditional sweet made for birthday celebrations in Brazil. Morgana explains that there is a strict rule: No sampling from the table of tempting desserts until the birthday song is sung and the cake is cut—no exceptions! Even harder than waiting? Trying to decide which flavor of bonbon is more delicious: the Brigadeiro (chocolate) or the Beijinho (coconut; variation below).

1 (14-ounce/396-g) can sweetened condensed milk

⅓ cup (80 ml) crème de leite or heavy cream

¼ cup (25 g) unsweetened cocoa powder, or more to taste

1 cup (115 g) chocolate sprinkles

1 tablespoon unsalted butter, at room temperature

1. Heat the condensed milk, crème de leite, and cocoa powder in a medium pan over medium heat and cook until the mixture thickens enough that the spoon leaves a streak along the pan, about 12 to 15 minutes.

2. Transfer the mixture to a bowl, cover, and refrigerate for 20 to 30 minutes, until completely cool.

3. Pour the sprinkles into a bowl or baking dish. Place 24 mini cupcake liners on a serving plate.

4. Rub a little butter on your hands, then scoop up about a teaspoon of the chocolate mixture and roll it into a 1-inch (2.5-cm) ball. Roll it in the chocolate sprinkles and place it in a cupcake liner. Repeat for the remaining 23 bonbons. Chill for 30 minutes before serving. Store any leftovers in an air-tight container for up to one week.

MORGANA'S BEIJINHOS
(Coconut Bonbons)

Replace the cocoa powder with 1 cup (85 g) unsweetened finely shredded coconut flakes (add more to taste). Follow the steps above, cooking for only 5 minutes in step 1, and chill for 15 minutes to make approximately 30 beijinhos.

MORGANA OLIVEIRA SOARES SPILLER

CENTRAL & SOUTH AMERICA | *Minas Gerais, Brazil*

Havana, Cuba

ANGELA DÍAZ PORTA

Angela Díaz Aranalde was born
in Havana, Cuba, and grew up during a
time when the revolution in Cuba was
becoming increasingly dangerous.

UNCERTAIN LIVING CONDITIONS AND THE need for freedom made many Cubans flee, leaving everything they knew and cherished behind in order to protect themselves and their families. In 1960, Angela's family decided to leave the island that had been home to their family as far back as she could remember. They settled in Brooklyn, where they took any available jobs to support themselves—Angela found a job in the medical records department of a hospital. When it became clear that they would not be returning to Cuba, they worked together to create stable, successful lives in the United States.

In 1965, she met her husband, Anibal Porta, also a Cuban exile, at a party. They married two years later and moved to Riverdale, New York, where their two daughters, Micaela and Gabriela, were born. Ten years later, the family moved to Connecticut, where they would see their girls through school, college, and marriage.

In addition to working in the medical profession, Angela dabbled in bookkeeping, real estate, retail, and also found her way to professional cooking by working for a café and catering company. Eventually, she joined her family's business, P. Jamas, a sleepwear company, where she handled customer service. Through it all, she still cooked for her family every night. She'd walk in, drop her keys, and begin to prepare the meal. One night her daughter had a friend staying for dinner. After Angela came in and immediately began to cook, the friend asked, "Does your mom always cook wearing her coat and purse?"

Angela often cooks traditional Cuban food for her daughters and now her grandchildren. For Angela's daughters, who grew up hearing about life in Cuba from their parents, grandparents, and extended family and friends, the food prepared in their home was a big part of their own Cuban-American identity. Certain dishes were for every day, others for special occasions. In conversation, people might compare how dishes were made differently according to each family's preferences. "Everyone says their mother's black beans are the best," says Angela's daughter Micaela, "but my mom's really happen to be *the best*."

Angela is quick to point out that when she first married, she couldn't cook at all. Since her husband could only make steak, she knew if she wanted to eat something else, she had to learn—quick. "I learned to cook because I love to eat," she explains, and it became clear her husband's limited repertoire wasn't going to suffice. Over the years she has taken cooking classes, studied and tested hundreds of recipes, and amassed a collection of cookbooks that she reads the way others read novels. But the recipes she turns to again and again are the ones she knows by heart—the ones her family carried with them from Cuba.

Angela's Ropa Vieja

serves 6 TO 8 | *PREP* 15 MINUTES | *TOTAL* 2½ HOURS, PLUS OVERNIGHT

THIS SHREDDED BEEF dish is a staple on the traditional Cuban table. In Spanish, the name translates to "old clothes," as the shredded meat resembles a saucy pile of rags. Commonly made with flank steak, Angela prefers a lean brisket for hers. Once ready to serve, Angela slices a pimento into thin strips and uses it to decorate the meat in a beautiful pattern. She also fries up some crusty bread to serve alongside—it's a great vehicle for sopping up that delicious sofrito!

½ cup (120 ml) fresh lime juice (about 2 limes)

1 small onion, thinly sliced

½ teaspoon coarse salt

½ teaspoon freshly ground black pepper

½ teaspoon garlic powder

½ teaspoon dried oregano

½ teaspoon ground cumin

2½ pounds (1.2 kg) lean-cut brisket

½ cup plus 2 tablespoons (150 ml) vegetable oil

1½ cups (360 ml) dry white wine

1 large onion, thinly sliced

1 large green bell pepper, thinly sliced

2 garlic cloves, smashed into a paste

6.5-ounce (184-g) jar fancy pimentos, 2 pureed or finely chopped and 1 sliced into thin strips (Angela prefers Goya)

1 (8-ounce/227-g) can tomato sauce

1 (8½-ounce/240 g) can small peas (Angela prefers Le Sueur)

2 bay leaves

1 large baguette, sliced into 1-inch (2.5-cm) slices

1. Combine the lime juice, onion, salt, pepper, garlic powder, oregano, and cumin in a large bowl.

2. Place the brisket in a large glass baking dish or plastic storage bag and pour the marinade over it; cover and refrigerate overnight.

3. Remove the meat from the marinade and dry with paper towels. Reserve the marinade.

4. Preheat the oven to 350°F (175°C).

5. Heat 2 tablespoons of the vegetable oil in a large Dutch oven over medium heat, then add the brisket. Brown on both sides, 2 to 3 minutes per side. Add the reserved marinade, ¾ cup (180 ml) of the white wine, and enough water to cover, 2 to 3 cups (480 to 720 ml).

6. Cover and place in the oven. Cook until fork-tender, 2 hours. At the 1-hour mark, check and add more water if the meat is no longer submerged.

7. Remove the meat from the cooking liquid and onto a cutting board. Discard the cooking liquid. Shred the meat with two forks.

8. *While the meat cooks, make the sofrito.* Heat 5 tablespoons (75 ml) of the vegetable oil in a large sauté pan over medium heat, then add the onion and cook until it begins to soften, 5 to 6 minutes.

Continues

9. Add the green pepper and cook until it begins to soften, 5 minutes.

10. Add the garlic, pureed pimentos, remaining ¾ cup (180 ml) wine, tomato sauce, half of the peas, and the bay leaves. Bring the mixture to a boil, then reduce to a simmer, cover, and simmer on low for 15 minutes.

11. Remove the cover, add the shredded meat and the other half of the peas, and simmer for 10 more minutes.

12. While the meat simmers, prepare the fried bread. Heat 3 tablespoons of the vegetable oil in a large sauté pan over medium-high heat, then add the bread slices and cook until golden brown, 1 to 2 minutes per side.

13. Serve on a platter topped with the sliced pimento and the bread around the outside of the platter.

Angela at her sister's wedding reception in May 1981.

Angela's Cuban Black Beans

serves 10 TO 12 | *PREP* 15 MINUTES | *TOTAL* 3 HOURS AND 15 MINUTES, PLUS OVERNIGHT

ANGELA COOKS MANY delicious dishes, but I have to agree with her eldest daughter, Miki: Her black beans are *the best*! Most often served with rice, this dish is simple yet spectacular. These beans are magic for a number of reasons, but the main one is that they have only a few ingredients but have a depth of flavor that is truly incredible.

2½ pounds (1.2 kg) dried black beans

2 lbs (907 g) green peppers (about 5 or 6), 1 cored and left whole with the remainder chopped, medium dice

2 cups (480 ml) extra-virgin olive oil (Angela prefers Spanish olive oil)

2 large yellow onions, diced

6.5-ounce (184-g) jar fancy pimentos, pureed in a food processor (Angela prefers Goya)

3 tablespoons plus 1 teaspoon coarse salt

½ teaspoon freshly ground black pepper

⅓ cup (80 ml) apple cider vinegar

1. Combine the black beans, whole green pepper, and about 12 cups (2.8 L) water, enough to cover the beans by 2 inches (5 cm), in a large stockpot. Soak overnight.

2. Bring the beans to a boil in the soaking liquid, then reduce the heat, partially cover with the lid, and simmer for 1 hour. Check the beans periodically, skimming any foam that forms.

3. *While the beans simmer, make the sofrito.* Heat 1 cup (240 ml) of the olive oil over medium heat, then add the onions and diced green peppers and cook until the onions are translucent and the peppers are soft but not browned, mixing periodically, about 20 minutes. Add the pureed pimentos and simmer for 5 minutes. Remove from the heat and puree the entire mixture in a food processor in batches until smooth.

4. After the beans have been cooking for an hour, test them—they should be soft but not fully cooked.

5. Remove the whole pepper from the beans and stir in the pureed sofrito. Simmer, partially covered, for 1 hour.

6. Stir in ⅓ cup (80 ml) of the olive oil and simmer for 15 minutes, then add another ⅓ cup (80 ml) of the oil. Simmer for another 15 minutes, then add the remaining ⅓ cup (80 ml) oil.

7. Stir in the salt, pepper, and vinegar and cook for another 30 minutes.

8. Serve immediately or cool completely and keep in the fridge or freezer until ready to use, up to 30 days. Angela usually makes her beans a few days in advance, and they taste better with each day that passes.

Angela's Boniatillo
(SWEET POTATO PUDDING)

serves 6 | **PREP** 15 MINUTES | *TOTAL* 1 HOUR AND 15 MINUTES, PLUS CHILLING IN REFRIGERATOR

THIS DESSERT, A sweet potato pudding, is quintessentially Cuban. Angela serves it in very small cups at the end of a meal because it's very sweet—a little goes a long way!

2 large Caribbean white sweet potatoes (about 2 pounds/907 g), peeled, trimmed of black spots, and cut into 1-inch (2.5-cm) pieces (see Note)

2 teaspoons coarse salt

1 cinnamon stick

Peel of 1 lime (2 strips the entire circumference of the lime)

Juice of ½ lime (about 1 tablespoon)

1½ cups (300 g) granulated sugar

4 large egg yolks

¼ cup (60 ml) dry sherry

1 tablespoon unsalted butter, melted

Ground cinnamon, to taste

Note

You can't substitute traditional sweet potatoes for this recipe and achieve the same results. White sweet potatoes are sometimes hard to find, but I was able to buy some at Whole Foods. They can also be found at Caribbean delis.

1. Combine the sweet potatoes with 1 teaspoon of the salt and enough water to cover in a large pot. Bring to a simmer and cook until the potatoes are fork-tender, about 30 minutes.

2. While the potatoes simmer, heat the cinnamon stick, lime peel, lime juice, sugar, and 2 cups (480 ml) water in another pot over medium-high heat, gently stirring to combine and dissolve the sugar. Bring to a boil and cook to create a syrup, 10 minutes. Set aside to cool for 10 minutes.

3. Strain the cooked sweet potatoes and place in a food processor with the warm syrup. Process until thick, smooth, and combined, working in batches if necessary.

4. Pour the sweet potato puree into the large pot and cook over medium heat, stirring constantly, until bubbles begin to form, about 5 minutes. Reduce the heat to low and continue stirring until the mixture comes away from sides of the pot, about 5 more minutes.

5. Add the egg yolks to a small bowl. Mix a small amount of the sweet potato into the egg yolks to temper them. Slowly add the egg yolks to the pot of sweet potato puree, stirring until fully combined. Cook for 5 minutes over low heat.

6. Stir in the sherry and butter and cook for 2 more minutes.

7. Transfer to a bowl, cover, and chill in the refrigerator for at least 1 hour.

8. Serve in small dessert glasses, dusted with ground cinnamon.

ANGELA DÍAZ PORTA

*Reparto Peralta Bella Vista Santiago,
Dominican Republic*

MARIA CRUZ

MARIA CRUZ WAS BORN IN the Dominican Republic and came to the United States with her family at the age of sixteen. She has lived in East New York for most of her life, working in factories and clothing stores. With her husband, Concepcion Chavez, she raised four children, Denise, Jennifer, Vanessa, and Luis, all while juggling multiple jobs. Raising four children in East New York was not easy. As Luis explains, his mother was always worried about him and his sisters getting caught up with the wrong friends and dangerous influences. Every day, the children were instructed to go straight to their father's deli after school, so as to learn a strong work ethic and to stay out of trouble.

Regardless of how tough the streets were and or how uneasy they sometimes felt at school, at home the children took comfort in the loving family they had. No matter what jobs she was working, Maria would always make sure to be home to greet her children when they returned from school or an after-school job with a delicious, hot dinner waiting on the counter. She felt it was important to teach her children how to make these cherished family recipes themselves, so they would always have a slice of home at their fingertips, no matter where they landed.

After raising her four children and working hard, she now spends her days at home, tending to her eight grandchildren and feeding them the foods of her family.

Maria's Mangú

(FRIED EGGS WITH SALAMI, CHEESE, AND PLANTAINS)

serves 4 | **PREP** 15 MINUTES | *TOTAL* 30 MINUTES

IF YOU EVER frequent a predominately Dominican neighborhood, you will see signs for *mangú* (boiled green plantains) in the windows of most of the local breakfast spots. The presentation is known as *los tres golpes*, meaning "the three hits": eggs, salami, and *mangú*. With red onion as a topping, it's a very hearty and colorful breakfast dish.

4 green plantains, peeled and halved lengthwise

Queso de freír (Maria prefers Tropical brand)

3 tablespoons mayonnaise

1 cup (2 sticks/227 g) unsalted butter

1 teaspoon coarse salt, plus more to taste

2 tablespoons vegetable oil

1 large red onion, sliced thin

Juice of 1 lemon

8 slices hard Dominican salami (Maria prefers Higueral brand)

8 eggs

1 avocado, sliced

1. Place the plantains in a large pot with enough cold water to cover. Bring to a boil over medium-high heat and cook until fork-tender, about 10 minutes. Remove the plantains from the water, reserving the cooking liquid.

2. Slice 8 thin slices of the queso de freír. Set aside.

3. Mash the plantains to a fine paste with a potato masher in a large bowl. Add the mayonnaise, butter, and salt to taste. In order to get the right consistency, add a bit of the reserved cooking liquid, ⅛ cup (30 ml) at a time, until a chunky paste is achieved. Set aside.

4. Heat 1 tablespoon of the vegetable oil in a small pan over medium heat, then add the onion and lemon juice. Cook until the onion is soft but not brown, about 5 minutes. Add a pinch of salt to taste. Transfer to a plate and set aside.

5. Wipe out the pan and heat 1 teaspoon of the vegetable oil over medium heat. Place the cheese slices in the pan without overlapping and cook until golden brown on both sides, about 1 minute per side. Transfer to a plate.

6. Place the salami in the pan and cook until golden on each side, about 30 to 40 seconds per side. Transfer to a plate.

7. Fry all of the eggs over easy or sunny-side up, depending on personal preference.

8. To plate, mound the plantains in the center of each dish. Lay 2 slices of cheese and 2 slices of salami around the plantains. Finish with 2 eggs and a spoonful of the fried onions on top.

Maria's Sancocho

(MEAT STEW)

serves 8 TO 10 | *PREP* 30 MINUTES | *TOTAL* 2 HOURS AND 15 MINUTES

WITH A LARGE extended family, Maria knows how to cook for a crowd. Her son, Luis, always jokes that Dominicans only know how to cook large amounts of food—Maria doesn't bat an eye when she needs to cook for more than twenty guests! *Sancocho* is typically made at their home as a celebratory meal. This is a true BIG crowd-pleasing dish—with loads of meats and a variety of vegetables, there is something for everyone in this pot!

1 pound (455 g) pork ribs

1 pound (455 g) beef neckbone

1 pound (455 g) chicken drumsticks

3 tablespoons adobo seasoning

3 tablespoons dried oregano

3 tablespoons garlic powder

Juice of 3 limes

½ cup (120 ml) Mojo marinade (Maria prefers Goya brand)

3 tablespoons canola or other neutral oil

4 chicken bouillon cubes

3 stalks celery, diced large

½ large onion, sliced

½ green bell pepper

½ bunch (about ½ cup/ 25 g) cilantro

1 yucca, peeled and cut into 1-inch (2.5-cm) pieces

1 carrot, peeled and cut into 1-inch (2.5-cm) pieces

1 kent pumpkin or butternut squash, peeled and diced

3 green plantains, peeled and cut into 1-inch (2.5-cm) pieces

1 teaspoon coarse salt

2 ears corn, husked and cut into ½-inch (12-mm) coins

1. Combine the pork, beef, and chicken with 1 tablespoon each of adobo, oregano, and garlic powder; the juice of 2 limes; and ¼ cup (60 ml) of the Mojo marinade in a large bowl. Cover and refrigerate for at least 30 minutes or up to 1 hour.

2. Heat the oil in a very large stockpot over medium-high heat. Remove the meat from the marinade. Working in batches, brown the meats for 4 to 5 minutes on all sides.

3. Return all the meat to the pot and add the bouillon cubes, celery, onion, green pepper, and the cilantro plus enough water to cover. Bring to a boil, then reduce to a simmer, cover, and cook for 1 hour.

4. Add the rest of the vegetables, except for the corn.

5. Add 2 tablespoons each of adobo, oregano, garlic powder; the salt; the remaining ¼ cup (60 ml) Mojo marinade; and the juice of one lime. Add more water, if needed, until all of the vegetables are covered by liquid.

6. Stir the contents carefully and lay the corn coins on top. Increase the heat and bring to a boil, then reduce to a simmer, cover, and cook the stew until the vegetables are fork-tender and the meat is falling apart, about 40 more minutes.

MARIA CRUZ

Pétion-Ville, Haiti

NIKITA "NIKKI" THÉODORE

◆

NIKITA "NIKKI" THÉODORE CAME TO the United States in the mid-1980s to explore New York City, the art world, and French literature and to discover a new, exciting life. She eventually settled in Brooklyn with her son, Olivier, and has called it home ever since.

Her apartment is beautifully decorated with colorful Haitian art, relics, and pictures of her adorable grandsons and family that remind her of her homeland. Although Nikki lives in the United States, the smells of her family's recipes are truly transporting. She often thinks of a proverb she learned from her mother: "It's the hand that cooks the dish." I find this to be so true, as the human touch—our life experiences, love, and emotions—are real ingredients when we cook. Food and the memories created while eating can truly transport you to your past, a special time in your life, or even to another place. Nikki cherishes the favorite dishes her mother and grandmother cooked for her as a child, and to this day, she has continued cooking these dishes for her own son and grandsons, despite being so far from home.

Nikki's Diri Djondjon

(RICE WITH DJONDJON MUSHROOMS)

serves 4 TO 6 AS A SIDE DISH | *PREP* 15 MINUTES | *TOTAL* 1 HOUR AND 15 MINUTES

DIRI DJONDJON, a very popular rice dish from Haiti, is unique in both taste and color. Djondjon mushrooms are native to northern Haiti, and they provide the base for this delicious dish. Interestingly, you don't eat the mushrooms; instead, the caps are steeped for the black juice they release in hot water. It's the juice that provides the flavor and color of the rice.

In Haiti, cooks usually make this dish with par-boiled rice, like Uncle Ben's. But Nikki prefers brown jasmine rice, so she adapted it from the original. Because par-boiled rice cooks much quicker than brown jasmine, you will need to cut the cooking time in half if you go the traditional route.

2 cups (70 g) dried djondjon mushrooms (see Note)

3 tablespoons extra-virgin olive oil (Nikki's preference), or any neutral oil (traditionally used)

2 scallions, chopped fine

2 garlic cloves, minced

1 cup (145 g) fresh peas or frozen lima beans (optional)

2 teaspoons kosher salt

2 teaspoons freshly ground black pepper

2 sprigs fresh parsley

1 teaspoon fresh thyme leaves

1 Scotch bonnet (optional)

2 cups (360 g) brown jasmine rice

1. Heat 3¾ cups (900 ml) water in a pot over high heat until boiling. Place the mushrooms in a heatproof bowl, then pour the boiling water over the mushrooms. Set aside for 15 minutes.

2. Heat 2 tablespoons olive oil in a large pot over medium heat, then add the scallions and garlic. If you are including the peas or lima beans, add them with an additional tablespoon of olive oil and cook, stirring, for about 10 minutes. If you are not adding peas or lima beans, cook the scallions and garlic until they soften but do not brown, 2 to 3 minutes.

3. Drain the mushrooms, reserving the soaking liquid, then press the mushrooms in a fine-mesh sieve to release as much water as possible. The mushrooms can be discarded, as they no longer retain flavor, or a few can be added as a simple garnish to the dish when adding the water. Make sure you still have about 3¾ cups (900 ml) water. If necessary, add a bit more water. Pour the liquid into the pot with the scallions and garlic.

4. Add the salt, pepper, parsley, thyme, Scotch bonnet (if using), and rice.

5. Bring the water to a boil, then reduce to a simmer, cover, and cook until the rice is cooked, 45 minutes.

6. Remove from the heat and let sit, covered, for 10 minutes for the flavors to meld.

Note

Because djondjon mushrooms are found only in Haiti, you will have to source them. Sam's Caribbean carries them and ships nationwide! www.sams247.com

Nikki's Poul Ak Nwa

(CASHEW CHICKEN)

serves 6 | **PREP** 30 MINUTES | *TOTAL* 1½ HOURS, PLUS OVERNIGHT

CASHEWS ARE THE most popular nut in Haiti, and with good reason—Cap-Haitian, located on the northern coast of Haiti, is home to one of the largest cashew farming communities in the world. Because of this, raw cashews are cooked with lots of different foods, including rice, fish, meats, veggies, and even hot chocolate in the north of Haiti. Cashew chicken is a signature regional dish eaten all over Haiti. Haitians also enjoy eating food with a spicy kick: Scotch bonnets are the pepper of choice, and they can be very hot. Nikki usually puts one in the pot and says she never knows how spicy it will be. If it's a bit on the mild side, sometimes she'll add a bit of hot sauce to give it the right level of heat. Her son Olivier says, "the hotter, the better." Removing the seeds will downplay the spice, so I'll leave that up to you.

1 (2- to 3-pound/907-g to 1.4-kg) whole chicken, cut into 8 pieces

Juice of 2 limes

Juice of 1 sour orange (see Note)

4 tablespoons extra-virgin olive oil

1 tablespoon stone-ground mustard

1 tablespoon white vinegar

1 tablespoon kosher salt

3 medium onions, 1 sliced thin and 2 diced small

1 garlic clove, minced

1 Scotch bonnet pepper, chopped, seeds removed (optional)

2 whole cloves

4 sprigs fresh parsley

2 plum tomatoes, diced small

2 small red bell peppers, diced small

1 small carrot, diced small

1 teaspoon tomato paste

¼ cup (60 ml) hot water

1 tablespoon dried thyme

1 tablespoon kosher salt

2 scallions, white and green parts chopped thin, or a few sprigs of chives

1 cup (120 g) raw cashews

Cooked white or brown long-grain rice

Note

Sour oranges are often used for making marinades and sauces in Haitian and Caribbean dishes. However, they may be difficult to source, so Nikki recommends combining the juice of 1 orange and 2 limes to mimic the flavor, if needed.

1. Rub the chicken pieces with the lime juice, then rinse the pieces in hot water. Place the rinsed chicken in a large, glass baking dish.

2. Pour the sour orange juice over the chicken. Add 2 tablespoons of the extra-virgin olive oil, the mustard, vinegar, and salt and rub over all of the chicken.

3. Add the sliced onion, garlic, Scotch bonnet to taste, cloves, and parsley.

4. Cover and refrigerate at least 1 hour or overnight (the longer the better).

5. Remove the chicken from the marinade, brushing the marinade off. Reserve all the marinade.

6. Heat the remaining 2 tablespoons extra-virgin olive oil in a large Dutch oven over medium heat, then add the chicken pieces, a few at a time, and brown on all sides. Remove to a plate. Drain all but 1 teaspoon of fat from the pot.

7. Add the diced onion, tomatoes, red pepper, and carrot to the pot and cook over medium heat until soft but not brown, about 5 minutes, then stir in the tomato paste and hot water.

8. Add the thyme, salt, scallions, and the reserved marinade to the pot. Lower the heat and simmer for 10 minutes.

9. While the vegetables simmer, combine the cashews and 1 cup (240 ml) water in a small pot. Bring to a boil and cook until only ¼ cup (60 ml) of the water remains and the cashews have become soft, 5 to 7 minutes.

10. Return the chicken to the pot with the vegetables. Add the cashews with their water. If needed, add additional water to cover the chicken.

11. Cover and simmer over medium heat for 40 minutes.

12. Serve with rice, spooning plenty of the spicy sauce over top, as Haitians do.

NIKITA THÉODORE

179

JANET PATRICIA LEZAMA

Unlike many American immigrants, Janet was an American citizen before she ever stepped foot on United States soil.

BORN IN MONTERREY, MEXICO, TO a Mexican father and an American mother, Janet grew up watching her Missouri-born mother, a respected doctor, learn how to speak Spanish and adopt Mexican traditions in their home. These memories would help her later in life when she became an immigrant herself.

Janet describes her family as loving and also quite big: She is the sixth of seven children. She never shied away from helping her mother in the kitchen, and by the time she was a teenager, she and her sister took charge of the nightly meals, much to her father's delight. Instead of meals with her mother's American flair, Janet preferred to cook authentic Mexican dishes; her father very much enjoyed his daughters' ability and deep interest in preparing the food of his, and their, homeland.

After high school, Janet went to college in Monterrey to study marketing. She married and began working in banking to help support their growing family of four children: Jesus, Patricia, Ana, and Gerardo. In time, her husband received a promotion that required a permanent relocation to New York. While moving to the United States may not have been part of her original plan, Janet was thrilled to move because, while she loved her life in Mexico, she knew her children would be afforded opportunities in the United States that Mexico could not offer, specifically concerning their education.

While Janet loved her new life, she did feel pressure to learn English quickly lest she and her children feel more unwelcome in their new surroundings. She missed how accepting the Mexican people were, how friendly and fraternal. However, with each passing day, they assimilated to their new lives, and she has seen her children grow and prosper.

Janet loves the freedoms of the United States and also how diverse it is. She is also incredibly proud of her children's success. While her children came here as young Mexican immigrants, they are now adults who went to excellent universities and have gone on to respected professions in highly competitive fields. They all appreciate their Mexican roots, even though the youngest two have little memory of life in Mexico. And they all love when Janet prepares their family's recipes for them—the same dishes she served her father so many years ago.

Janet's Huevos Divorciados

("DIVORCED EGGS")

serves 1 | **PREP** 15 MINUTES | *TOTAL* 25 MINUTES

THIS DELICIOUS BREAKFAST dish is "divorced" due to the fact that each egg is topped with a different salsa. The dish is comprised of perfectly cooked over-easy eggs, one enrobed in salsa verde while the other swims in salsa roja, and you won't know which one to dig into first. Janet whips up her quick, easy homemade salsas for this dish (recipes follow), but you can substitute with store-bought salsa if you want.

½ cup plus 1 teaspoon (125 ml) vegetable oil

2 large eggs

2 corn tortillas

Kosher salt, to taste

Freshly ground black pepper, to taste

Salsa Roja (page 184)

Salsa Verde (page 184)

½ avocado

1. Heat 1 teaspoon of the oil in a small, nonstick frying pan over medium heat. Crack the eggs into the pan and cover with a lid until the whites set but the yolks are still runny, 2 minutes.

2. Heat the remaining ½ cup (120 ml) vegetable oil in a separate small pan over medium heat, until shimmering, and drop in one of the corn tortillas. Fry for 1 minute on each side, just to soften. Drain on paper towels and sprinkle with salt and pepper to taste. Repeat for the other tortilla.

3. To plate, place one egg on top of each tortilla. Top one egg with salsa roja and the other with salsa verde. Garnish with the avocado.

Janet's Salsa Roja

makes 2 CUPS (480 ML) | *PREP* 10 MINUTES
TOTAL 20 MINUTES

10 small or 5 large red tomatoes

4 garlic cloves, peeled

2 small serrano peppers or jalapeños, cored and seeded (optional, see Note)

1 teaspoon kosher salt

1 teaspoon vegetable oil

1 white onion, minced

1. Core the tomatoes and puree them with the garlic, peppers, if using, and salt in a blender.

2. Heat the oil in a large pan and cook the onion until soft and translucent, about 8 minutes.

3. Add the tomato mixture and cook, stirring, until heated through and combined, 10 minutes. Cool and serve or freeze for up to 30 days.

Note

You can use either serrano peppers or jalapeños for this recipe, but Janet prefers serranos. She says they are great for aiding in digestion.

Janet's Salsa Verde

makes 3 CUPS (720 ML) | *PREP* 20 MINUTES
TOTAL 40 MINUTES

10 tomatillos, husks removed

2 small serrano peppers or jalapeños (optional, see Note)

1 bunch (¾ cup/45 g) cilantro, stems removed

4 garlic cloves, peeled

3 teaspoons kosher salt

2 tablespoons vegetable oil

1 large white onion, minced

1. Combine 4 cups (960 ml) water, the tomatillos, and the peppers, if using, in a large pot and bring to a boil. Cook until the tomatillos change color and begin to soften and crack, 15 minutes.

2. Remove the peppers from the water and remove their stems. Reserve the water. Puree the tomatillos and peppers with the cilantro, garlic, salt, and 2 cups (480 ml) of the cooking water in a blender.

3. Heat the vegetable oil in a large saucepan over medium heat, then cook the onion until translucent, about 8 minutes. Add the tomatillo mixture and cook, stirring, until the salsa thickens slightly (note that this is a thin salsa), 10 to 15 minutes. Cool and serve or freeze for up to 30 days.

Janet's Refried Beans

makes 3 CUPS | PREP 5 MINUTES | TOTAL 1 HOUR AND 40 MINUTES, PLUS OVERNIGHT

THESE BEANS TASTE great with rice or as an accompaniment to Pork Tamales (page 187).

1 pound (455 g) pinto beans, soaked overnight (see Note)

½ cup (105 g) shortening or lard

1 teaspoon kosher salt, plus more to taste

Note

Janet makes her refried beans in a pressure cooker so that she doesn't have to soak them, significantly reducing prep time. To cook these in a pressure cooker, place the dried beans (unsoaked) in the bowl of the pressure cooker with enough water to just cover, and cook them under high pressure for 25 to 30 minutes. Proceed to step 3.

1. Drain the beans and place them in a medium saucepan with enough fresh water to cover.

2. Simmer the beans until they are very tender, 1 hour or longer. Let cool for 25 to 30 minutes.

3. Transfer the beans to a blender and puree for 5 minutes, until smooth.

4. Melt the shortening in a large sauté pan over medium heat. Add the pureed beans and the salt.

5. Cover and simmer until the mixture is very dry, about 40 minutes. Add salt to taste, if needed. Remove from the heat and serve immediately, or they can stand up to 1 hour, covered, until you are ready to eat.

Janet's Pork Tamales

serves — 12 TO 15 (MAKES 40 TO 50 TAMALES) | *PREP* 4 HOURS | *TOTAL* 6 HOURS

THIS RECIPE IS a true labor of love. To lighten the load, Janet will make the filling a few days earlier than she needs it so when it's time to fill the masa, she simply has to heat the pork up in a pan before stuffing the tamales. Janet's Refried Beans (page 185) can be used as an optional filling.

FOR THE PORK FILLING

3 pounds (1.4 kg) pork butt, cut into 2-inch (5-cm) pieces

½ large white onion, peeled

1 tablespoon plus 2 teaspoons kosher salt

1 tablespoon freshly ground black pepper

2 large ancho chiles (dried poblano chiles, about 3 ounces/85 g)

40 to 50 corn husks

FOR THE MASA

1⅓ cups (275 g) refined pork lard

4 cups (520 g) instant masa

2 teaspoons baking powder

2 teaspoons kosher salt

1. *Make the pork filling.* Combine the pork with the onion, 1 tablespoon of the salt, the pepper, and 6 cups (1.4 L) water. Bring to a boil, then reduce to a simmer and cook, partially covered, for 3 hours.

2. While the pork simmers, combine the ancho chiles and 1 cup (240 ml) water in a pot, bring to a boil, and cook for 30 minutes. Remove the chiles from the water, reserving the cooking liquid, then remove their stems and seeds. Puree the chiles in a blender with ¼ cup (60 ml) of the cooking liquid. Set aside.

3. When the pork is done (it will be fork-tender), remove it from the water and shred with two forks. Reserve 4 cups (960 ml) of the pork broth.

4. Combine one-third of the pureed ancho chiles, the remaining 2 teaspoons salt, ¼ cup (60 ml) of the reserved broth, and the shredded pork in a large pot over medium heat and cook to meld the flavors, 4 to 5 minutes. Remove from the heat and set aside.

5. Soak the corn husks in hot water until soft, 15 to 20 minutes, while you make the masa.

6. *Make the masa.* Beat the lard in a large stand mixer with the paddle attachment or with an electric hand mixer on high until it becomes very fluffy, at least 10 minutes. Set aside.

7. Combine the rest of the ancho chile puree with the masa, baking powder, salt, and approximately 3½ cups (840 ml) of the reserved broth in a large bowl. Mix by hand until a sticky dough forms, adding more broth, a few tablespoons at a time, if too dry.

Continues

8. Turn the stand mixer back on low speed and slowly add small amounts of the hand-mixed dough to the lard. Mix until the dough has a paste-like consistency, 2 to 3 minutes.

9. Remove the corn husks from the water and wring them dry. Lay them on a towel and arrange similar-sized husks together for consistent tamales.

10. Place one husk upright in the palm of your hand. Spoon and spread the masa paste on the bottom half of the husk in a very thin layer. Add 3 to 4 tablespoons of pork filling, depending on the size of the husk, and fold the husk into a tamale (see right). Tie a strip of extra husk around it to hold it closed. Repeat for the rest of the masa and filling.

11. Place 4 cups (960 ml) water in a large steamer pot. Line the bottom of the steamer insert with small and broken pieces of corn husk. Layer the tamales on top, arranging them side by side in one direction, then in a different direction for the next layer, to promote the flow of steam.

12. Place a small dish atop the tamales, then cover with a tea towel. Cover with the lid and steam for 1 hour. Turn off the heat and let sit, covered, in the steamer for 1 hour.

13. Serve with Refried Beans (page 185) and Salsa Verde (page 184).

JANET PATRICIA LEZAMA

Spoon and spread the masa paste into
an upright husk in the palm of your hand,
then add the pork filling.

Fold the sides of the corn husk
in over the filling.

Then, fold the bottom of the corn husk up
to create a small packet.

Tie a strip of extra husk around the packet to
hold it closed. If using more than one filling,
the ties can be used to differentiate them.

SHEILA BRATHWAITE HAIRE

As a young girl in Panama, Sheila knew she was destined to live in the United States, even though her childhood in Panama had been pleasant.

SHE WAS RAISED PRIMARILY BY her maternal grandparents, and her grandfather James was an esteemed employee of the Panama Canal Company. Born and college-educated in Barbados, he applied and was accepted into an office-level job, a position immigrants and people of color were often unable to obtain. As a perk of employment, residence and schooling was included for the children of Panama Canal employees. Because of the international influence there, the zone was a comfortable place to live, and the schools were academically superior to those in other areas of the country. James, valuing education, made sure his children excelled in school and guaranteed three of his children positions in the office of the zone as well.

At the time, children and grandchildren of Panama Canal employees were granted passage to the United States without much difficulty. Sheila was an adventurous and curious young woman and yearned for new experiences, so at the age of sixteen, she packed her bags and said goodbye to her Panamanian life. By the time Sheila left, many of her family members had already immigrated, though some she met for the first time when she arrived in Brooklyn with her beloved grandmother Icelda, who traveled with her. There Sheila was taken in by her cousin Barbara and commenced high school.

Sheila's grandparents were a constant positive force in her life. Both were immigrants to Panama—James from Barbados and Icelda from Jamaica. Sheila's grandmother was like a second mother to her, her siblings, and all her cousins. Icelda was always in the kitchen cooking dishes from her native Jamaica as well as the Bajan dishes her husband enjoyed as a child. Comforting, home-cooked meals were shared and enjoyed by their big, boisterous family on a daily basis. Everyone showed up when her grandmother made toto, a Jamaican quick bread chock-full of coconut and raisins. With many Bajans and Jamaicans immigrating to Panama to work on the canal, neighbors and friends appreciated the homeland foods coming out of the Brathwaites' kitchen. Sheila's childhood acquaintances will still approach her, forty years after her grandmother's passing, to rave about the food her grandmother prepared for them.

When Sheila first arrived in the United States, she did not know how to cook. As the youngest of all the grandchildren, she had been a bit pampered by all her elders. But, if she wanted to eat before her cousin Barbara's late-night arrival from work, she would have to learn. Her fiery spirit and determination kicked in. She worked with her family members to piece together her talented grandmother's recipes and began to master them all, one by one.

Family means everything to Sheila. Her strong family network always rallied around her in times of need, helping her raise her daughter, Nichole, now a successful pediatrician, and also giving her a strong foundation that has served her well her entire life. When her beloved son-in-law passed away in the 9/11 attacks in 2001, it was Sheila's turn to be there for her family. After this devastating loss, she began to commute weekly to her daughter and two grandchildren, Jassiem and Nia, to help them maintain a routine and cope. Whether it was preparing a hot meal or giving a ride to soccer practice, no task was too big or too small. She just wanted her family to get on as best they could, and they came through these moments of sadness stronger because they were together.

Although she now lives on her own in Florida, she speaks to her family regularly to check in and make sure everyone is healthy and happy. Sheila still focuses on new experiences. Her strong, adventurous spirit continues to drive her, and she enthusiastically explains "I'm here, living my BEST life."

Sheila's Arroz con Pollo

(PANAMANIAN CHICKEN AND RICE)

serves 4 TO 5 | **PREP** 20 MINUTES | **TOTAL** 1 HOUR AND 25 MINUTES

SHEILA CALLS THIS her go-to dish. Her trick for cutting down on time is to make the rice in a rice cooker while cooking the chicken in the oven. According to Sheila, nothing is worse than overcooked rice, so she loves how the rice cooker gives her perfect rice every time. She sets it and forgets it as she works on her savory, flavor-packed sofrito.

3 pounds (1.4 kg) skin-on, bone-in chicken thighs, trimmed of excess fat and halved

½ teaspoon kosher salt

½ teaspoon freshly ground black pepper

1 tablespoon garlic powder

1 tablespoon onion powder

1 teaspoon paprika

1 teaspoon adobo seasoning

1 teaspoon crushed red pepper flakes, plus more to taste

3 tablespoons extra-virgin olive oil

1 cup (190 g) jasmine rice, rinsed

¼ teaspoon Bijol seasoning

2 garlic cloves, minced

½ medium yellow onion, chopped fine

½ packet sazon con culantro y achiote (Sheila prefers Goya)

½ cup (75 g) alcaparrado manzanilla olives (Sheila prefers Goya)

1. Preheat the oven to 350°F (175°C).

2. Combine the chicken thighs with the salt, pepper, garlic powder, onion powder, paprika, adobo, and red pepper flakes in a large bowl.

3. Heat 2 tablespoons of the extra-virgin olive oil in a large Dutch oven over medium heat. Add the chicken thighs.

4. Cover, place in the oven, and cook until the chicken is cooked through and the juices run clear, 45 minutes to 1 hour.

5. **While the chicken cooks, make the rice.** Place the rice along with the amount of water called for in the package directions in a pot or rice cooker. Add the Bijol seasoning and stir gently to incorporate. Cook according to package directions, then set aside.

6. **Make the sofrito.** Heat the remaining 1 tablespoon extra-virgin olive oil in a medium sauté pan over medium heat, then add the garlic and onion and cook until the onion is semi-translucent and the garlic is lightly toasted, about 5 minutes. Add the sazon and stir to combine.

7. Add the olives with half of the juice from the jar and stir again. Remove from heat.

8. Remove the chicken from the oven and set aside.

9. Add the rice and sofrito to the Dutch oven and stir to combine. Add the chicken back into the pot and stir to combine again. Serve immediately.

SHEILA BRATHWAITE HAIRE

Sheila's Bajan Cou Cou

(CORNMEAL AND OKRA)

Serves — 4 TO 6 | *PREP* 10 MINUTES · | *TOTAL* 1 HOUR AND 10 MINUTES

COU COU IS the national dish of Barbados. That's probably why it's one of the first dishes Sheila's grandmother learned after marrying a Bajan man. Similar to polenta or grits, cou cou is traditionally served with salt cod or flying fish fried with onions and gravy. As you're cooking, remember to keep stirring! The Bajans call it "turned cornmeal" because you have to keep the cornmeal moving to prevent lumps. They even have a special wooden "cou cou stick" to turn it!

8 ounces (227 g) okra

2 teaspoons salt

1 cup (227 g) coarse-ground cornmeal

1 tablespoon salted butter

1. Remove the stems from the okra and cut into thin disks.

2. Combine the okra, 1 teaspoon of the salt, and 4 cups (960 ml) water in a medium pan, bring to a boil, and cook until the okra is very soft, 10 minutes.

3. Drain the okra, reserving the cooking liquid. Set aside.

4. Add the cornmeal to the same saucepan with 1 cup (240 ml) of the reserved liquid and heat over medium heat, stirring constantly and slowly with a straight-edged wooden spoon until the mixture begins to bubble.

5. Lower the heat, add the okra with 1 cup (240 ml) reserved cooking liquid, and simmer for 1 hour, stirring every few minutes. After about 1 hour, the cornmeal should be very soft and have no bite. If it begins to get too thick, add more of the reserved liquid, ¼ cup (60 ml) at a time.

6. Add the remaining teaspoon salt and the butter. Stir to combine. Serve immediately.

Sheila's Jamaican Toto

(SPICED QUICK BREAD)

makes ONE 9 × 5 × 2½ INCH LOAF | *PREP* 10 MINUTES | *TOTAL* 1 HOUR AND 10 MINUTES

THIS DELICIOUS QUICK bread was a favorite in Sheila's household. Filled with spices, coconut, and raisins, it tastes delicious fresh out of the oven with a little butter.

½ cup (1 stick/115 g) unsalted butter, at room temperature, plus more for greasing

1 cup (220 g) packed light brown sugar

2⅓ cups (290 g) all-purpose flour

1 teaspoon baking powder

¼ teaspoon ground nutmeg

1 teaspoon ground cinnamon

1 teaspoon vanilla extract

1 cup (85 g) dried grated coconut

1 cup (145 g) raisins

1. Preheat the oven to 350°F (175°C). Grease a 9 × 5-inch (23 × 12-cm) loaf pan.

2. Combine the butter and brown sugar in a large mixing bowl using a wooden spoon or electric hand mixer until fully combined.

3. In a separate bowl, whisk together the flour, baking powder, nutmeg, and cinnamon.

4. Add the flour mixture to the butter mixture and stir to incorporate.

5. Add the vanilla, coconut, and raisins and stir until fully combined.

6. Pour the mixture into the prepared loaf pan and bake for 1 hour, until the top begins to brown and crack.

ROCÍO QUISPE-AGNOLI

◆

ROCÍO QUISPE-AGNOLI IS A professor of Hispanic Studies at
Michigan State University. She loves her work and has always been very
passionate about her career in academia. This passion is what brought
her to the United States as a young student. Although she loves her
native Peru, after graduating from college she realized that she needed
to move to North America if she wanted to advance professionally. So
she applied for, and won, a fellowship to study at Brown University. She
excelled at her studies, worked hard, and realized her dream of becoming
a recognized scholar.

But despite her professional accomplishments, she has never
forgotten her roots. In Peru, the cuisine reflects the country's incredibly
diverse population and geography. Flavors come from Indigenous,
Mestizo, African, Asian, and European cuisines. Not surprisingly, the
country's three very distinct geographical features—coast, mountain,
and rain forest—contribute to the unusually wide variety of dishes
Peruvians eat. The result is a cuisine that is not only delicious but
unique. Rocío fondly remembers how the family conversations of her
childhood, especially those between her mother and grandmother, who
lived with her family, seemed to revolve around their interesting food.

Before leaving home, she had the foresight to copy her mother's
cherished recipe book, knowing she would need the comforts of her
mother's kitchen on her new journey. She never veers from her trusty
recipe book, so when she prepares her mother's dishes, she is confident
they are true to her family and will always taste like home.

Rocío's Causa

(LAYERED POTATO CASSEROLE)

serves 8 TO 10 | *PREP* 30 MINUTES | *TOTAL* 1 HOUR

THIS APPETIZER CAN be found in Peruvian restaurants. There, the layers are stacked in a round mold so that they can be displayed beautifully in the shop windows. At home, it is made in a slightly less decorative way in a large baking dish and cut into little rectangles. Either way, it's delicious!

3 pounds (1.4 kg) Yukon Gold potatoes

2 tablespoons olive oil

Juice of 2 limes (about 3 tablespoons)

¼ teaspoon hot red chili pepper paste, plus more to taste (Rocío prefers Sazon del Peru brand)

1 teaspoon coarse salt

1 teaspoon freshly ground black pepper

1 (7-ounce/200-g) can tuna packed in water, drained, or boiled shrimp or shredded chicken

1 cup (480 ml) mayonnaise

½ cup (75 g) marinated black olives, sliced

1 medium avocado, sliced

1 large egg, hard-boiled and sliced

1 small onion, minced

1 medium tomato, sliced

¼ cup (13 g) chopped parsley

1. Boil the potatoes in salted water until fork-tender, about 15 minutes. Peel the potatoes and mash them with the oil, lime juice, chili paste, salt, and pepper.

2. Divide the potato mixture into thirds. Evenly spread the first third on the bottom of a 9 × 13-inch (23 × 33-cm) glass baking dish.

3. Mix the tuna with the mayonnaise and evenly spread it on top of the potato layer. Top with half of the black olives.

4. Evenly spread the second third of the mashed potato on top of the olives. Layer the sliced avocado on top of the potato, followed by half of the sliced egg, and then the minced onion.

5. Evenly spread the final third of the potatoes on top and let the dish rest for 30 minutes. Top with the tomato, parsley, and the remaining half of the sliced egg and olives.

6. Slice into 4 × 3-inch (10 × 7.5-cm) rectangles and serve.

Rocío's Ceviche

PERUVIANS LOVE CEVICHE, a dish of fresh fish that is acid-cooked in lime juice and served with *choclo*, a delicious, large-kernel corn found all over Peru.

1 pound (455 g) sea bass or tilapia

Juice of 3 limes (about ½ cup/120 ml)

1 aji rocoto or other red chili pepper (seeds removed, if desired), finely chopped

¼ red onion, sliced thin

2 tablespoons parsley, chopped fine

1 teaspoon kosher salt

1 large sweet potato

4 green lettuce leaves

1 20-ounce (567-g) can choclo, drained (Rocío prefers Belmont Natural Foods brand)

1. Cut the fish into small, ¼-inch pieces and toss them with the lime juice, chili, and red onion in a bowl, ensuring the fish is coated in the lime juice.

2. Add the parsley and salt to the bowl. Mix, cover, and place the bowl in the refrigerator for at least 30 minutes.

3. Peel the sweet potato and cut into ¼-inch (6-mm) thick slices.

4. Place the sweet potato in a small saucepan with enough water to cover, bring to a boil, and cook until the sweet potato is fork-tender, 10 minutes. Drain and set aside.

5. Lay the lettuce on a serving platter. Arrange the sweet potatoes in a circle around the edge of the platter, on top of the lettuce. Place the fish in the middle of the plate.

6. Place two mounds of the choclo on both sides of the fish.

Rocío and her son, Jan.

Rocío's Pastel de Alcachofas

(ARTICHOKE TART)

serves 6 TO 8 | *PREP* 20 MINUTES | *TOTAL* 1 HOUR AND 10 MINUTES

ROCÍO'S MOTHER MADE this artichoke tart for very special occasions, like birthdays. She would cut it into squares, drizzle them with béchamel, and serve portions on fancy dessert plates. *Pastel de alcachofas* is delicious, decadent, and definitely worthy of any formal occasion (but it's perfect on a weeknight, too).

FOR THE TART

2 sheets (from a 14.1-ounce/399-g box) prepared pie crust

3 tablespoons unsalted butter

1 medium onion, finely chopped

1 small garlic clove, finely chopped (about 1 teaspoon)

1 (12-ounce/340 g) can artichoke hearts, drained and finely chopped

1 teaspoon coarse salt

1 teaspoon freshly ground black pepper

5 large eggs, 4 beaten and 1 hard-boiled

1¼ cups (300 ml) whole milk

6 tablespoons (37 g) grated Parmesan cheese

1 large egg yolk mixed with 1 tablespoon water, for egg wash

FOR THE BÉCHAMEL

2 tablespoons unsalted butter

2 tablespoons all-purpose flour

2 cups (480 ml) warmed whole milk

1 teaspoon kosher salt

1. Preheat the oven to 350°F (175°C).

2. *Make the tart.* Fit one of the pie crusts into the bottom of an 8 × 8-inch (20 × 20-cm) glass baking pan. Trim the crust to fit the pan.

3. Melt the butter in a large pan over medium heat, then add the onion and garlic and cook until the onion is transparent, about 5 minutes. Add the artichokes and cook until soft, another 3 to 4 minutes. Add the salt and pepper, stir, and remove from the heat to cool.

4. Mix the beaten eggs, milk, and Parmesan cheese in a bowl.

5. Combine the artichoke mix with the Parmesan cheese and the egg mixture, stirring well.

6. Pour the mixture into the prepared pie crust and add the hard-boiled egg (whole or cut in half).

7. Cover the filling with the second pie crust. Trim to fit the pan, then prick the top with a fork so steam can escape.

8. Brush the top with the egg wash, and bake for 45 to 50 minutes, until the top is a dark golden brown.

9. *Make the béchamel.* Melt the butter in a large sauce pan over medium heat. Add the flour and mix into a light roux, about two minutes.

10. Lower the heat and slowly whisk in the milk. Continue to cook until the mixture thickens enough to coat the back of a spoon.

11. Whisk in the salt and drizzle over each tart square to serve.

HAYDEE MARTINEZ

Haydee Martinez was born in a rural area of Humacao, Puerto Rico.

AS THE MIDDLE CHILD OF twelve, she was responsible for helping to care for her younger siblings, and Haydee often had a prominent role in cooking and working to help her large family survive.

When Haydee was only a teenager, her mother sent her to the United States mainland to help care for her older sister's children. Because Puerto Rico is an unincorporated territory of the United States, Puerto Ricans are thereby US citizens and are able to move freely between the island and the US mainland. Haydee arrived without a coat in the middle of a cold winter in New York, a place that was very different from the one she had always known.

Despite the fact that she knew very little English, she immediately began working to make a new life for herself, both as a live-in nanny for her sister's family and in various factory jobs. She had never driven a car, so she often walked to work regardless of the weather. A short time later, Haydee relocated to New Jersey to live with one of her brothers. As she began to explore and learn more about her new community, she happened upon a church that she heard offered events and classes. There, she met a priest who helped her to learn English and then to sew on a machine, which enabled her to find seamstress jobs with better pay, one of which had her sewing uniforms for the New York Yankees.

Haydee has always been fiery and independent, and she finds it hard to sit idle. These qualities make her the kind of person who refuses to tolerate injustice, and she quickly became an outspoken advocate for workers' rights at the factories where she was employed. She worked hard to engrain herself in the culture of her companies, and even with her limited English, she became a vocal component of her local unions, eventually heading up one of the women's workers unions at only twenty-one years old.

Once she had saved a bit of money and established herself in an apartment of her own, her mother, Julia, brought over Haydee's young daughter, Margarita, whom she had been caring for back in Puerto Rico. Throughout the years that followed, her apartment became a place of refuge for other family members who came to the States, including Haydee's youngest brother, who she raised alongside her own daughter. Haydee sent everything she could to help support her family that stayed behind. The cooking skills that she gained from preparing meals for her brothers and sisters as a child were honed by cooking for her often-full household of relatives who lived with her on and off for several years. To this day, she can turn any small handful of ingredients into a large, hearty meal with no notice or preparation.

Despite her busy schedule, Haydee found time to take classes at night and managed to amass a wide variety of certifications in different areas. A true jack-of-all-trades, Haydee has worked many different jobs in order to provide for her family—seamstress, beautician, cheesemonger, private investigator, nanny, taxi driver, hospice nurse—but she says that her favorite job by far has been her role as a grandmother and great-grandmother. Today, Haydee is the matriarch of a family of strong, empowered women (and one great-grandson). Her warm and generous caretaking spirit extends out from her family and into the community, where she works with local churches in Newark, New Jersey, helping to run food pantries that serve meals to the homeless.

Growing up, Haydee's family was not well-off, and she and her siblings often went without the food they needed. She recounts that meat, especially, was a scarcity that was only enjoyed at the holidays, if ever. Now, she relishes providing her family with all the food they could ever want, and takes special joy in preparing a large, traditional Puerto Rican feast for Christmas Eve every year.

Haydee's Arroz con Gandules

(RICE WITH PIGEON PEAS)

serves 6 TO 8 | **PREP** 20 MINUTES | **TOTAL** 1 HOUR AND 5 MINUTES

PUERTO RICANS HAVE their big Christmas meal on Christmas Eve (*Nochebuena*), and Haydee always makes a big pot of rice with pigeon peas for the occasion. She makes a nice, savory base for the rice by rendering the fat from a few small, fatty pieces of pork that she shaves off of the Pernil (page 208) before it goes into the oven.

If you want the coveted *pegao*, the crispy browned rice that sticks to the bottom of the pot as the rice steams to perfection, you have to be attentive when you mix it. For Puerto Ricans, it's as valuable as any gift under the tree!

1 pound (455 g) medium-grain white rice

2 tablespoons olive oil

¾ cup diced pork butt (approximately 1-inch/2.5-cm pieces) (optional)

¼ cup (35 g) finely chopped yellow onion

¼ cup (35 g) coarsely chopped red bell pepper

2 tablespoons coarsely chopped green bell pepper

2 garlic cloves, smashed

¼ cup (10 g) chopped cilantro (stems and leaves)

¼ teaspoon freshly ground black pepper

1½ teaspoons salt

1½ teaspoons capers

¼ cup (40 g) Manzanilla olives with pimentos, whole

8-ounce (227-g) can of tomato sauce

1 cup (145 g) green pigeon peas, drained

1. Rinse the rice until the water runs clear. Strain and set aside.

2. Heat the olive oil in a large pot over medium heat, then add the pork and cook until the fat begins to render and the meat browns.

3. Add the onion and cook until it is translucent, 5 minutes.

4. Add the bell peppers, garlic, and cilantro and cook until the peppers soften and the onion begins to brown, another 3 to 4 minutes.

5. Add the pepper, salt, capers, and olives and stir to combine.

6. Add the tomato sauce, rice, and 2 cups (480 ml) water (or enough to just cover the rice). Raise the heat to high and bring to a boil. Stir the contents of the pot a few times.

7. Reduce to a simmer, cover, and cook until the rice is al dente, about 25 minutes.

8. Remove the lid and stir in the peas. Cover and cook for 15 more minutes, or until the rice is tender.

Haydee's Pernil
(ROAST PORK BUTT)

serves 10 | *PREP* 10 MINUTES | *TOTAL* 7 HOURS, PLUS OVERNIGHT

PERNIL IS A HOLIDAY staple for many Puerto Ricans, and Haydee's family is no exception. She rubs it with the marinade the day before and then places it in the oven on Christmas Eve morning to be eaten later that evening. The result is tender, succulent, and absolutely delicious served with her Arroz con Gandules (page 207).

1 (7- to 8-pound/3.2- to 3.6-kg) bone-in pork butt

Juice of 3 sour oranges (see Note, page 177)

1 tablespoon minced garlic

½ teaspoon freshly ground black pepper

¼ cup (60 ml) white vinegar

2 tablespoons extra-virgin olive oil

2 tablespoons kosher salt

4 whole cloves

Cooked white rice

Fried plantains

1. Preheat the oven to 350°F (175°C).

2. Rub the pork with the sour orange juice in a large bowl, ensuring it is well coated in juice.

3. Combine the garlic, pepper, vinegar, olive oil, and salt in a small bowl. Set aside.

4. Remove the pork from the bowl and place on a large cutting board. Pierce the meat on all sides with a small knife.

5. Rub the pork with the garlic mixture, then place the cloves into a couple of the slits. Cover and refrigerate overnight.

6. Place the pork in a large roasting pan and bake for 6 to 7 hours. The meat should be very tender.

7. Slice and serve with rice (page 207) and fried plantains (opposite).

A photograph of young Haydee taken by a photographer who stopped her on the street in New York City. The string of pearls was one of the first items she purchased with money she earned working odd jobs.

Haydee's Plátanos Maduros

(FRIED SWEET PLANTAINS)

serves 6 TO 8 AS A SIDE DISH | *PREP* 5 MINUTES
TOTAL 10 MINUTES

3 very ripe yellow plantains (dark brown to black)

2 cups (480 ml) vegetable or canola oil

1. Peel and slice the plantains into ¼-inch (6-mm) rounds.

2. Heat the oil in a medium sauté pan over medium heat. When the oil begins to shimmer, add the plantain rounds to the pan making sure they do not overlap. The oil should just cover the rounds.

3. Cook until lightly browned, about 2 to 3 minutes per side. Remove from the pan with a spatula and transfer to paper towels to drain.

4. Repeat for the remaining plantains.

Haydee's Tostones

(FRIED GREEN PLANTAINS)

serves 6 TO 8 AS A SIDE DISH | *PREP* 10 MINUTES
TOTAL 20 MINUTES

3 green plantains

Coarse salt

2 cups (480 ml) vegetable or canola oil

1. Peel and slice the plantains on the bias into 1-inch (2.5-cm) diagonal pieces.

2. Mix 1 teaspoon salt into a medium bowl of room-temperature water. Add the plantain slices to a bowl and soak for 5 minutes. Drain.

3. Meanwhile, heat the oil in a medium sauté pan over medium heat. When the oil begins to shimmer, add the plantain slices to the pan making sure they do not overlap. The oil should just cover the slices.

4. Cook until lightly browned, about 2 to 3 minutes per side. Carefully remove the slices with a metal spatula to a cutting board or clean surface and smash each one down to ¼ inch (6 mm) thick with the bottom of a glass.

5. Return the slices to the pan and cook for an additional 2 to 3 minutes until crispy.

6. Remove from the pan with a metal spatula and transfer to paper towels to drain. Sprinkle with salt while still warm.

7. Repeat for the remaining plantains.

HAYDEE MARTINEZ

CENTRAL & SOUTH AMERICA | *Humacao, Puerto Rico*

"Shekaiba never forgot the family she left behind: 'I had the means to help so I had to make it happen.'"

—SHEKAIBA WAKILI BENNETT

PART FIVE

MIDDLE EAST

SHEKAIBA WAKILI BENNETT

Some people are simply
born with a passion.

FOR THOSE WITH THIS SPECIAL GIFT, they are able to see the world from the perspective of others and fight for justice and peace. This personality trait is strong in Shekaiba Wakili Bennett, an Afghani immigrant who came to the United States at ten years old. Her internal flame continues to ignite her ideas, her activism, and her fierce love for family.

Shekaiba, born in Kabul, clearly remembers the Russian invasion in 1979 and how her life completely changed overnight. Because of her father's career working for UNICEF, her family began to see friends and colleagues disappear, and life no longer felt safe or secure. One night, the Afghan communists came to her home, rousing her paternal uncle, Abdula, from bed at gunpoint. He was never seen again. Her father, Rahim, knew it was only a matter of time before he would also be imprisoned or killed, so he felt he had to do something quickly. Unlike many, however, he had a way out.

Because of his work, he was in possession of a valid US visa, so he requested a transfer to the New York City office. A transfer was granted, and he headed to New York to establish residency and begin to carve out a new life. A year later, he sent for his wife, Shekaiba's stepmother, and their daughters.

Shekaiba knew she was incredibly fortunate to get out of Afghanistan with her father's help. Unfortunately, due to her parents' divorce, her mother and youngest sister were left behind. She began her new life in Long Island, NY, but an important piece of her remained back in Afghanistan. Moving to New York was a life-changing opportunity. She was able to live freely and safely and attend school. It was not lost on her that while she was given the ability to prosper in the States, those still in Afghanistan were under the control of a terrible regime with no feasible resolution.

She graduated from high school with high marks and dedicated her college studies to earning a teaching degree. She also worked three part-time jobs: When she wasn't studying, she was waitressing, heading to work-study, and even working as a bank teller. She used any money she made to pay for her education and saved the rest to help get her family out of Afghanistan.

Shekaiba never forgot the family she left behind. She would watch the news in horror as she learned that the Taliban outlawed women from studying and began closing schools. Shekaiba's aunt Soraya was removed from her university simply because she was a woman. Shekaiba knew something had to be done.

With her ultimate goal being to bring her family to safety, she worked tirelessly to find a way out for them. No amount of red tape could deter her from obtaining an American life for her family. Conducting the work of an immigration lawyer, she began writing letters, filling out paperwork, and sending the required documents to the closest US embassy in the region, in Pakistan. She saved enough money to move her mother, sister, aunt, and uncle to a house in Pakistan where she knew they would be safe while she waited for their US visas to clear. She coordinated with both the United States and Pakistani governments until all the interviews were completed and the visas were granted.

While her uncle decided to remain in Pakistan, her mother, sister, and aunt were granted entrance to the United States, and have all since become US citizens. When I asked her why she refused to give up in spite of all of the administrative and political hurdles she faced, she replied, "because they were my family and what was happening to them was unjust. I had the means to help so I had to make it happen."

Shekaiba went on to complete a master's degree at Columbia University, marry her husband, Derek, and have two sons, Strider and Phoenix. She works actively to help new refugees in Connecticut, collecting clothes and furniture for refugee organizations. Her work helps those trying to build a new life just has she did so many years ago. Shekaiba is proof positive that if you shine enough love on a hateful situation, love will win.

Shekaiba's Palaw

(BEEF AND RICE WITH CARROT RAISIN DRESSING)

serves 6 | **PREP** 30 MINUTES | **TOTAL** 1 HOUR AND 30 MINUTES

MANY CONSIDER *KABULI* palaw, a meat and rice dish, the national dish of Afghanistan. It is traditionally prepared with lamb, but Shekaiba puts her own twist on it: She combines the recipe with another traditional dish, Potato Tahdig (page 216), by layering the bottom of the rice pot with potatoes, and she uses beef instead of lamb. These dishes take a bit of time—you can't begin making the rice until the beef is finished cooking because it's the savory cooking liquid that gives the rice its deep, rich color and flavor—but the extra time is worth it.

FOR THE MEAT

2 tablespoons olive oil

1 medium onion, finely chopped

2 pounds (910 g) beef chuck, rinsed and cut into 2-inch (5-cm) pieces

1 tablespoon tomato paste

1 teaspoon freshly ground black pepper

1 teaspoon ground coriander

1 tablespoon kosher salt

1 tablespoon garlic paste (see Note, page 216)

FOR THE TOPPING

1 cup (110 g) raw slivered almonds

1 cup (130 g) raw pistachios

1 cup (145 g) raisins

1 tablespoon vegetable oil

20-ounce bag of matchstick carrots or 2 medium carrots (6 ounces) cut into matchsticks

2 teaspoons sugar

Cooked jasmine rice (optional)

1. ***Make the meat.*** Heat the olive oil in a large pot over medium heat for 2 minutes, then add the onion and cook until translucent, 5 minutes.

2. Add the meat and cook, stirring, until browned on all sides, 5 to 7 minutes.

3. Add the tomato paste, pepper, coriander, salt, and garlic paste and stir to coat the meat. Add 3 cups (720 ml) water and bring to a boil.

4. Reduce the heat to low, cover, and simmer until the meat is tender, 1 hour.

5. ***While the beef simmers, make the topping.*** Place the nuts and raisins in a large colander and rinse with cold water.

6. Heat the vegetable oil in a large sauté pan over very low heat, then add the carrots and sugar and cook until the carrots are just softened, being careful not to brown, about 3 to 4 minutes.

7. Add the nuts and raisins to the pan and stir to combine. Set aside.

8. When the beef is fork-tender, remove it and reserve 2 cups (480 ml) of the liquid to use in the Potato Tahdig (page 216), if making.

9. To serve in the traditional way, spoon the cooked beef over a platter of jasmine rice and top with the carrot mixture. Serve immediately. To serve as Shekaiba does, make Potato Tahdig (page 216).

Shekaiba's Potato Tahdig

(SCORCHED POTATO AND RICE)

serves 6 | **PREP** 30 MINUTES | *TOTAL* 1 HOUR AND 30 MINUTES

4 tablespoons (60 ml) extra-virgin olive oil

1 large Russet potato, peeled and sliced thin

2 cups (360 g) basmati rice

2 cups (480 ml) beef broth (ideally reserved from the beef in making the Palaw, page 214)

2 cups (480 ml) hot water

2 tablespoons kosher salt

1 teaspoon ground cardamom

1 teaspoon ground cumin

1. Pour 1 tablespoon of extra-virgin olive oil into a rice cooker, and then place the potato slices in an even layer across the bottom.

2. Spread the rice over the potatoes, careful not to disturb the layer.

3. Combine the beef broth and 2 cups (480 ml) hot water with the salt, cardamom, cumin, and the remaining 3 tablespoons oil and carefully pour the mixture over the rice. Cover the pot with a tea towel, then the rice cooker lid, and cook for 1 hour, until the rice is cooked and fluffy.

4. Spoon the rice onto a large platter, careful to leave the bottom 2 inches (5 cm) of rice undisturbed.

5. Using a large dish, flip the remaining rice over so that the potato bottom is now on top. This is known as the potato tahdig and can be served separately from the rice.

6. You can serve as is, or do as Shekaiba does and spoon the cooked beef from the Palaw (page 214) over the rice and top with the carrot mixture. Serve immediately.

Note Shekaiba likes to buy peeled garlic in bulk and grind it up with a bit of oil in a food processor. She keeps a jar of the homemade paste in her fridge because she uses it in so many dishes. You can also buy premade garlic paste or substitute finely minced garlic.

Shekaiba's Bolani

(FRIED POTATO AND SCALLION TURNOVERS)

makes 14 | **PREP** 20 MINUTES | *TOTAL* 35 MINUTES

IN AFGHANISTAN, A thin flatbread is prepared for these fried turnovers, but Shekaiba found that store-bought pizza dough is a very close substitute and saves time. Her children love them, and the dipping sauce is a must. In Afghanistan, they are made with a variety of fillings; Shekaiba's family favorite is this simple potato and onion combination.

FOR THE BOLANI
2 large russet potatoes, washed and peeled

1 tablespoon extra-virgin olive oil

15 scallions, thinly sliced

1 teaspoon salt

½ teaspoon freshly ground black pepper

½ teaspoon ground coriander

2 (20-ounce/570-g) prepared pizza doughs

¼ cup (60 ml) vegetable oil

FOR THE DIPPING SAUCE
1 cup (240 ml) whole-milk Greek yogurt

½ English cucumber, grated and squeezed to remove excess water

1 teaspoon salt

1 teaspoon dried mint

1. *Prepare the bolani.* Cut the potatoes into ½-inch (12-mm) discs and place them in a medium pot. Cover the potatoes with cold water. Bring to a boil and cook until fork-tender, about 15 minutes.

2. Heat the olive oil in a medium sauté pan over medium heat, then add the scallions and cook until they have softened, about 7 minutes. Add the salt, pepper, and coriander, and stir to combine. Remove from the heat and set aside to cool.

3. Drain the potatoes and mash until smooth. Fold in the scallions until fully combined.

4. Cut each pizza dough into 7 small balls. Roll each out to ½ inch (12 mm) thickness and cut with a 2-inch (5-cm) biscuit cutter or a drinking glass.

5. Place 3 tablespoons of the potato mixture in the center of each disk and fold over to enclose the filling, pinching to seal the half-moons.

6. Heat the vegetable oil in a large cast iron skillet over medium heat.

7. Place four of the pockets into the hot oil and fry until golden, 2 to 3 minutes per side. Drain on paper towels. Repeat with the remaining pockets.

8. *Make the dipping sauce.* Combine the yogurt, cucumber, salt, and mint in a small bowl. Serve alongside the bolani.

LUCY YERANOSSIAN

◆

LUCY YERANOSSIAN WAS BORN IN Beirut to Armenian parents. Her mother, Mariam, had fled to Lebanon from Turkey as a child after her parents perished in the Armenian Genocide in 1915. Like many other displaced cultures, Lucy's family valued the heritage of their homeland and made sure to keep it alive at home by speaking Armenian and cooking and eating their beloved dishes. Although their legacy was in Armenia, they also began to assimilate to life in Lebanon, learning Lebanese dishes and embracing their new culture. Lucy became fluent in Arabic and French, and once she decided to move to the United States, she enrolled at American University in Beirut to study English as well.

Upon arrival, she joined her sister Anahid in Queens and found work at a bank. She married her husband, Karl, and they went on to have three children: Christine, Danny, and Peter. Eventually, they decided to leave city life behind and settled in nearby Pearl River, New York.

After spending twelve years at home raising her children, Lucy parlayed her interest for antiques and fine pottery into a thriving business. She started small, opening a stall in the local mall, but managed to grow her business into three standalone shops around New York. Her children even joined her at her stores after school and on weekends.

Lucy is a fabulous home cook who creates many Middle Eastern favorites for her children and grandchildren. Her grandchildren adoringly call her "Mama," short for "Medz Mama," which is Armenian for "grandma" or "big mama." The name certainly fits—anyone who meets her knows that her heart and love for her family is most definitely *medz* . . . BIG!

Lucy's Sini Kufteh

(BEEF AND POTATO CASSEROLE)

serves 6 TO 8 · | **PREP** 30 MINUTES | **TOTAL** 1 HOUR AND 25 MINUTES

LUCY LOVINGLY REFERS to this delicious casserole of beef and potatoes as "Armenian Shepherd's Pie." This dish is so easy to put together—the ground beef doesn't need to be cooked before baking—and has a secret ingredient (ketchup!), a change Lucy made to the original recipe when she discovered her love for the condiment.

1 cup (240 ml) vegetable oil

4 medium roasting potatoes (about 2 pounds/907 g), peeled and sliced into ¼-inch (6-mm) rounds

2 pounds (907 g) ground beef (90 percent lean)

½ cup (25 g) chopped parsley

1 medium onion, finely chopped

1 teaspoon freshly ground black pepper

1 teaspoon allspice

1 teaspoon coarse salt

⅓ cup ketchup

2 beefsteak tomatoes, thinly sliced

1. Heat the oil in a large pan over medium heat, then place potato slices in the oil in one layer and fry until light golden brown, about 4 minutes. Flip the potatoes and cook for another 2 to 3 minutes; the potatoes should still be firm. Drain on paper towels and set aside. Repeat with the remaining potatoes until they are all cooked.

2. Preheat the oven to 425°F (220°C).

3. Combine the ground beef, parsley, onion, pepper, allspice, salt, and ketchup in a large mixing bowl.

4. Evenly spread the meat mixture in a 9 × 13-inch (23 × 33-cm) baking dish.

5. Lay the potato slices in rows on top of the meat, overlapping slightly. Repeat with the tomato slices.

6. Cover the dish with aluminum foil and bake for 45 minutes. Remove the foil and bake for 10 more minutes. The potatoes and tomatoes will be lightly golden brown when done.

Lucy circa 1960.

Lucy's Hummus

makes 3 CUPS | PREP 15 MINUTES | TOTAL 15 MINUTES

LUCY'S HUMMUS IS a hot commodity. Her family requests it for all their gatherings, and if her daughter Christine goes to a dinner party, her friends won't let her in the door without it. It's by far the best hummus I've ever tasted—it's really hard to go back to the grocery store variety after you try this. And, it's so easy, you never have to!

According to Lucy, when eating hummus, you should *never* dip your pita into the communal hummus. Her mother taught her that the gluten in the pita will ruin the taste of the hummus you leave behind. Do as the Armenians do—spoon some hummus into your dish and dip away!

1 (1-pound, 13-ounce/ 822-g) can chickpeas, drained, with 1 cup (240 ml) liquid reserved (see Note; Lucy prefers Goya)

½ cup (120 ml) tahini, mixed if separated

¼ teaspoon coarse salt

2 garlic cloves, chopped

Juice of 2 lemons (about ¼ cup/60 ml)

Pitted black olives

Chopped parsley

Extra-virgin olive oil

Pita bread

1. Place the chickpeas, tahini, salt, half of the garlic, and half of the lemon juice in a food processor. Pulse for 2 minutes.

2. Scrape down the sides and taste. Add more of the lemon juice or garlic as desired. Pulse to incorporate.

3. To serve, scoop the hummus onto a large serving dish. Arrange the olives around the edge of the dish and sprinkle the hummus with chopped parsley and a drizzle of oil. Serve with pita bread.

Note

If your saved hummus thickens overnight, you can stir in a few tablespoons of the reserved chickpea liquid to bring it back to your desired consistency.

Tip

Take your leftover hummus and mix in some plain Greek yogurt and lemon juice to make a great dip for veggies or dressing for salad!

Lucy's Karni Yarek
(MEAT-STUFFED EGGPLANT)

serves 6 TO 8 | *PREP* 20 MINUTES | *TOTAL* 1 HOUR AND 10 MINUTES

LUCY RAISED HER three American kids on all the delicacies of *her* mother's Armenian kitchen, like this stuffed eggplant dish. Much to the chagrin of her eggplant-hating children, this recipe was always on regular rotation in Lucy's home. (They still shudder at memories of eggplants roasting on an open flame every Sunday morning!) To appease them, she would substitute some of the eggplant with tomatoes and green peppers so that everyone would eat dinner.

10 small (about 4 ounces/115 g each) eggplants

2 cups (480 ml) canola oil

1 pound (455 g) ground beef (85 percent lean)

1 small onion, chopped

⅛ teaspoon allspice

⅛ teaspoon freshly ground black pepper

1 teaspoon coarse salt

½ cup (65 g) pine nuts (Lucy prefers pine nuts from Turkey)

1 (14.5-ounce/411-g) can diced tomatoes

1. Preheat the oven to 400°F (205°C).

2. Leaving the stem of the eggplants intact, and starting at the top, peel strips down to the bottom, creating a stripe pattern.

3. Heat the oil in a large pot or Dutch oven over medium-high heat. Place the eggplants in the pot, ensuring the oil reaches halfway up the eggplants.

Cook until the outsides are dark brown on each side, 5 to 8 minutes per side. Depending on the size of your pot, you may need to do this in batches. Remove the eggplants from the oil and place on paper towels to drain.

4. Remove the oil from the pot, reserving 2 tablespoons.

5. Heat 1 tablespoon of the reserved oil in the same pot over medium heat. Add the beef and cook, stirring, until brown, about 8 minutes. Drain the beef and set aside. Add the second tablespoon of reserved oil and cook the onion until softened, 5 to 6 minutes. Add the cooked beef, allspice, pepper, and salt to the pot, stirring to combine.

6. Remove the pot from the heat and add the nuts.

7. Place the eggplants in a 9 × 13-inch (23 × 33-cm) baking dish. With a paring knife, cut a deep slit into each eggplant without going all the way through. Fill each eggplant with 3 to 4 tablespoons of the meat filling.

8. Spoon the diced tomatoes with the juices around the eggplants and add ½ cup (120 ml) water so that the bottom of the pan is moist with tomatoes and water.

9. Bake for 45 to 50 minutes, until the vegetables are fork-tender.

Lucy's Bulgur Pilaf

serves 6 | **PREP** 5 MINUTES | **TOTAL** 20 MINUTES

THIS RECIPE IS a common side dish in Lucy's home. Bulgur is high in fiber and the thin pasta adds a soft, nutty taste to the dish. It comes together quickly and is a great accompaniment to both meat and fish dishes, but Lucy makes it most often to serve alongside her Karni Yarek (page 222).

2 tablespoons unsalted butter or Crisco, plus more as desired

1 cup coarse bulgur wheat

½ cup (75 g) vermicelli pasta, gently crumbled

2½ cups (600 ml) chicken broth, heated slightly

Coarse salt

Freshly ground black pepper

1. Melt the butter or Crisco in a medium pot over medium heat. Add the bulgur and crumbled pasta and cook until the pasta browns and smells nutty, about 3 minutes.

2. Add 2 cups (480 ml) of the chicken broth and bring to a boil. Cover, reduce to a simmer, and cook until all the broth is absorbed and the bulgur has softened, about 15 minutes. If you prefer the bulgur to be a bit softer, add the remaining ½ cup (120 ml) chicken broth incrementally, until it is as soft as you wish.

3. Remove from the heat and season with salt and pepper to taste. Stir in more butter (about 2 tablespoons) for a creamier texture.

4. Fluff before serving.

Lucy celebrating Thanksgiving, November 1970.

SHARAREH "SHARI" OVEISSI

◆

SHARI NEVER IMAGINED A TIME in her life when she would not live in Iran. She has beautiful memories of enjoying the countryside and playing with her siblings in the mountains. Her father, Mostafa, was both a respected general and a Renaissance man who loved to paint and sculpt, and who taught his daughter about art and gardening. Shari loved spending time with him tending his vegetables and observing how he loved nature. Shari's mother, Mahin, is the matriarch of the family. Having a strong foundation in the arts and music was important to the Sarmads, so Shari grew up appreciating her cultural studies. Both of Shari's parents guided her in the kitchen, and she credits them with giving her the skills she needed for raising her own family.

Shari's life was content. She married, started a family, and had two boys. While maintaining a happy home life, she knew it was also important to continue her studies, so she completed university, graduating with a degree in art.

In 1978, due to her husband's position in the military and the political climate at the time, remaining in Iran became impossible. For the safety of her family, Shari had to leave the country she loved and move to Paris. Once settled, she enjoyed all France had to offer, but Shari dreamed of the day she would return to her beloved homeland.

Unfortunately, tragedy struck soon after—her husband died unexpectedly. Leaving everything behind once again, she resettled in the United States and created a new life as a single mother. Once the boys were in school, she pursued her own interests by earning another degree, this time in interior design. She also became a realtor to combine her loves of art, design, and architecture. She now has grandchildren with whom she loves to spend her time.

Cooking Persian food and preserving the religious and cultural practices she grew up with is very important to Shari. She cherishes her knowledge of the dishes of her youth and enjoys how her cultural traditions gather her family around the table. They remind her of the Iran she left, the childhood she loved, and the country that will always remain in her heart.

Shari's Fesenjoon

(WALNUT AND POMEGRANATE STEW)

serves 4 | **PREP** 10 MINUTES | *TOTAL* 1½ HOURS

THIS STEW, CALLED *fesenjoon*, is quite popular in Iran. Made with ground walnuts and pomegranate molasses, the thick, nutty sauce has a unique sweet-and-sour quality that beautifully flavors the chicken. Typically, it is made in the colder months of the year, when pomegranates are in season and readily available in the market. Be sure to serve it over a bed of rice or Shari's Tahdig (page 228), as the rice sops up the sauce so well.

¼ cup (60 ml) vegetable oil

1 large onion, minced

1 teaspoon turmeric powder

2 pounds (907 g) skinless, bone-in chicken thighs and breasts

1 tablespoon coarse salt

1 teaspoon freshly ground black pepper

2 cups (190 g) walnut halves

1 cup (240 ml) pomegranate molasses

2 tablespoons sugar, or more to taste

Seeds of one pomegranate

1. Preheat the oven to 350°F (175°C).

2. Heat the oil in a large pot over medium-high heat, then add the onion and cook until it begins to soften, 5 minutes.

3. Add the turmeric and cook, stirring, until the onion is light brown, 5 more minutes.

4. Add the chicken and season with salt and pepper. Brown the chicken on both sides, about 3 minutes per side. Add enough water to just cover the chicken. Bring to a boil, then cover, reduce the heat, and simmer until the chicken is cooked through, 40 minutes.

5. While the chicken simmers, bake the walnuts on a baking sheet 8 to 10 minutes, until toasted and aromatic. Cool, and then grind the walnuts in a food processor until they become a paste.

6. Add the walnut paste, pomegranate molasses, and sugar to the pot with the chicken and stir to incorporate. Taste—it should have a sweet and sour flavor, but if you would like it a bit sweeter, then add up to 2 tablespoons more sugar. Simmer covered, stirring occasionally, until the stew has thickened, 20 to 30 more minutes. If the stew becomes too thick, add a little water. If it's too runny, remove the lid and allow some water to evaporate until the stew reaches your desired consistency.

7. Place the stew in a serving bowl and sprinkle the pomegranate seeds on top.

Shari's Tahdig

(SCORCHED RICE)

serves 8 TO 10 | *PREP* 10 MINUTES | *TOTAL* 1 HOUR

WHEN IRANIANS MAKE this dish, there is one very important component: the bottom, which ultimately becomes the top! *Tahdig*, or "scorched rice," is the beautiful golden crust created at the bottom of the pot during a special cooking process. After parcooking the rice, Shari smears a layer of fat on the bottom of the pot and returns the rice for another steam, where a crispy, almost fried layer is created. Seasoned and colored with beautiful threads of saffron, there is simply nothing like it. As Shari explains, Persian cooking is a matter of practice and skill. Personally, I found that using a nonstick pot really helped achieve the results I was looking for without the rice sticking to the bottom. It may take a few tries to achieve a perfect golden crust, but when you do, it will be worth it.

FOR THE SAFFRON WATER

¼ cup (60 ml) hot water

3 pinches of saffron

FOR THE RICE

4 cups (720 g) basmati rice

1 tablespoon coarse salt

4 teaspoons saffron water

3 tablespoons Greek full fat yogurt

½ cup (120 ml) vegetable oil

1 tablespoon unsalted butter, melted, or more to taste

1. *Make the saffron water.* Combine the water and saffron and let steep until the water turns red and the saffron wilts. Do not remove the wilted saffron. Set aside.

2. *Make the rice.* Place the rice in a bowl with enough cold water to cover. Stir vigorously and then drain. Repeat 3 or 4 more times, until the water runs clear.

3. Place the washed rice in a large nonstick pot (nonstick is very important) and add the salt and enough water to just cover. Bring the water to a boil, then reduce to a simmer, cover, and parcook until the rice is still somewhat firm and there is still some water in the pot, 10 minutes. Drain the rice and remove to a separate bowl. Set aside.

4. Combine the saffron water, yogurt, and the vegetable oil in the same pot as the rice, spreading to coat the bottom of the pot.

5. Top the yogurt mixture with the drained rice. Using the handle of a wooden spoon, poke holes along the top of the rice (about ½ inch deep) to allow steam to escape. Drizzle the melted butter over the rice.

SHARAREH OVEISSI

6. Heat the pot over low heat. Drape a dish towel over the pot and then cover with the lid and simmer for 40 minutes.

7. Increase the heat to high and cook for 2 minutes to ensure a golden brown crust.

8. Remove from the stove and carefully scoop out the loose rice with a large spoon, avoiding the hardened rice at the bottom. Use a rubber spatula to carefully peel the crust from the bottom of the pot and place it over top of the loose rice. Serve with Fesenjoon (page 227).

SHARAREH OVEISSI

229

SCHEHERAZADE "CHERIE" JAFAR

◆

CHERIE JAFAR WAS BORN IN London, England, to a British mother and an Iraqi father. At the age of three, her family moved to Baghdad, Iraq, for seven years. Then, she returned to her country of birth, but this time to Bath, to study. At nineteen, she married and headed to the United States as a young bride.

Because of her diverse background, Cherie is versed in a number of different cuisines. She cooks dishes from her native lands, England and Iraq, but she also makes a number of Lebanese dishes taught to her by her mother-in-law. She keeps a small recipe book with dishes from all over the world. She can throw together an authentic tabbouleh to start, a Middle Eastern stew as a main, and then finish the meal with an English bread pudding.

Cherie explained how she loves gathering her family for American Thanksgiving, now her favorite holiday. "Every immigrant can enjoy this holiday. It's a celebration without religious ties or presents. The goal is simply to enjoy food and family. Everyone celebrates it—no one is excluded." Her daughters Layla, Nadia, and Neda look forward to this celebration every year because it reminds them of their childhood.

Her daughter Layla explained that when they were young, Cherie always cooked more than was needed for dinner each night—the table was always covered with a number of delicious dishes and ended with a healthy salad. And like any mother from any culture, Cherie always insisted her children eat some.

Cherie's Tabbouleh

(BULGUR AND PARSLEY SALAD)

serves — SERVES 8 TO 10 AS AN APPETIZER (MAKES 5 CUPS/1.2 L) | *PREP* 1 HOUR | *TOTAL* 3 HOURS

TABBOULEH IS A staple side dish in the Middle East. It tastes delicious on its own or with pita bread. Cherie's version has an extra-lemony kick!

½ cup (70 g) bulgur wheat

5 packed cups (250 g) Italian flat-leaf parsley

½ cup (120 ml) olive oil

⅓ cup (80 ml) lemon juice (from 2 to 3 large lemons)

½ teaspoon coarse salt, or more to taste

Freshly ground black pepper

2 large tomatoes, seeded and diced small

6 scallions, chopped fine (white parts and lowest 1 inch/2.5 cm of green)

1. Rinse and drain the bulgur wheat. Place it in a bowl and refrigerate for 1 hour to soften.

2. While the bulgur rests, pick all the parsley leaves. Wash them thoroughly and place in a salad spinner to completely dry. Chop finely (you will have about 2 cups chopped).

3. Whisk together the olive oil, lemon juice, salt, and pepper in a large bowl. Add the bulgur, parsley, tomatoes, and scallions and stir to combine. Season with additional salt to taste.

4. Cover and refrigerate to further soften the bulgur and let the salad absorb the flavors of the liquids, 1 to 2 hours.

Note

Sometimes Cherie likes to include cucumber in this dish. If you'd like to do the same, chop 1 Persian cucumber into small dice and add it to the mix, along with 2 to 3 more tablespoons lemon juice to taste.

Cherie's
Kousa Mahshi
(STUFFED ZUCCHINI)

serves — 6 | *PREP* 30 MINUTES | *TOTAL* 1 HOUR AND 25 MINUTES

KOUSA MAHSHI MEANS "stuffed squash." Cherie made this dinner dish, popular in many parts of the Middle East, for her family often. Cherie uses a zucchini corer to create a well to perfectly stuff the savory meat and rice mixture into the vegetable. My recipe tester Monita found that an apple corer can be used, but you have to insert it from both ends of the zucchini because it's not as long. A variation of this dish is kousa bil-laban, where you top the zucchini with plain yogurt, crushed garlic, and salt rather than a tomato-based sauce.

FOR THE ZUCCHINI

6 medium zucchini

2 tablespoons olive oil

1 small onion, minced

½ pound (227 g) ground beef (85 percent lean)

1 teaspoon ground cinnamon

1 teaspoon allspice

1 teaspoon ground nutmeg

¼ cup (45 g) basmati rice, rinsed until the water runs clear

FOR THE SAUCE

1 tablespoon olive oil

1 small onion, minced

1 garlic clove, chopped

1 beefsteak tomato, sliced ¼-inch (6-mm) thick

⅓ cup (80 ml) tomato paste

2½ cups (600 ml) warm water

1¼ teaspoons dried mint flakes, crushed

1 tablespoon coarse salt

1. Prepare the zucchini. Trim and core the zucchini and set aside. Save the cores to make the bonus recipe at right (see Tip).

2. Heat the olive oil in a large pot over medium-high heat, then add the onion and cook until brown, about 8 minutes. Remove the onion to a large bowl and set the pot aside without cleaning.

3. Add the beef, spices, and rice to the bowl with the onion and mix to combine.

4. Roll small amounts of the mixture with your hands and stuff the zucchini. To ensure you have filled the middles, gently tap one end on the counter to level the mixture. Once they are all filled, set aside.

5. Make the sauce and cook the zucchini. Heat the oil in the same pot over medium heat, then add the onion and cook until translucent, about 5 minutes, being careful not to brown. Add the garlic and cook until just softened, 1 to 2 minutes more. Layer the tomato on top of the onion to cover the bottom of the pot. Place the stuffed zucchini into the pot atop the tomatoes.

6. Combine the tomato paste and warm water, whisking until the tomato paste has dissolved. Add the dried mint and salt and pour the mixture over the zucchini.

SCHEHERAZADE JAFAR

MIDDLE EAST | *Baghdad, Iraq / Bath, England*

7. Cover and bring to a boil, then lower the heat and simmer until the zucchini is fork-tender, 45 to 55 minutes.

8. Remove the zucchini to a serving plate. Place an immersion blender into the pot and blend up the cooked tomato mixture. Season to taste and pour the sauce over the zucchini.

Tip

Never one to let food be wasted, Cherie made us a delicious little appetizer with the cored zucchini pulp while we waited for the Kousa Mahshi to cook. Simply boil the cores for 5 minutes, drain them, then combine with ½ white onion, grated; ¼ cup (60 ml) olive oil; ¼ cup (60 ml) red wine vinegar; 1 tablespoon crushed dried mint; and the juice of half a lemon. Pour it all on top of some toasted pita bread and garnish with additional fresh mint.

SCHEHERAZADE JAFAR

MIDDLE EAST | *Baghdad, Iraq / Bath, England*

Cherie's Bamia

(LAMB AND OKRA STEW)

serves 6 | **PREP** 10 MINUTES | **TOTAL** 1½ HOURS

THIS DELICIOUS LAMB stew is perfect for a cold winter night. The addition of okra and tamarind paste gives it a unique flavor and makes for a hearty, one-pot wonder.

1½ pounds (683 g) lamb stew meat, cut into 2-inch (5-cm) chunks

Coarse salt

Ground white pepper

2 tablespoons extra-virgin olive oil

¼ cup (60 ml) tomato paste

6½ to 7 cups (1.5 to 1.7 L) chicken stock

2 (1.5-pound/670-g) jars pointed okra, drained (Cherie uses Tamek brand with the tomatoes removed)

6 garlic cloves, peeled

1 teaspoon tamarind paste or ½ cup (120 ml) lemon juice

1. Season the lamb with salt and white pepper.

2. Heat the olive oil in a large pot over medium-high heat and cook the lamb until brown on all sides, 2 to 3 minutes per side.

3. Add the tomato paste and enough chicken stock to cover the meat (about 4 cups/960 ml). Bring to a boil, then reduce to a simmer and cook, uncovered, for 45 minutes.

4. Add the drained okra, garlic, and the remaining chicken stock to cover. Cook for 20 more minutes.

5. Add the tamarind paste and cook for 5 more minutes.

IRENE FARHI SANKARI

◆

IN JANUARY OF 1962, IRENE came to the United States with her parents from Beirut, Lebanon, and settled in Buffalo, New York. She was seven years old. With a Syrian mother and an Egyptian father, she grew up in a multicultural home where the main language was French. Even after moving to the United States, her mother insisted Irene study French, and the tradition continues—Irene and her husband, Jack, speak only French at home, and when they started their own family, Irene took comfort in cooking traditional foods passed down from her own mother. While she loves to cook for her children, Andrea, Michael, and Dina, when they visit, her true passion is painting. Her home is filled with her portraits, still lifes, and other amazing pieces.

When talking about her transition to the American way of life, Irene explained how when her family first moved here, no one even knew what pita bread was: "We had to eat Wonder bread," she said. She remembers having to travel all the way to Sahadi's in Brooklyn to get Middle Eastern specialties like stuffed grape leaves for the holidays. "Now you can get hummus in fifty different flavors!" she exclaimed.

Irene's Kibbeh
(BEEF CROQUETTES)

serves 4 TO 6 (MAKES 16) | PREP 30 MINUTES | TOTAL 1 HOUR

KIBBEH IS A quintessential Middle Eastern mezze. The traditional version is made with a savory meat filling and a bulgur shell, but this variation is made with a bulgur and flour shell. The kibbeh have a football-like shape, and the trick to achieving this is to form the dough into perfect little spheres and then pull out the edges. As Irene explained, it is important that your kibbeh are uniform for presentation. She invested in a meat grinder accessory for her standing mixer so that even her filling is uniform! Serve them with hummus (such as Lucy's Hummus, page 221) for dipping.

FOR THE FILLING

2 tablespoons canola oil or other neutral oil

1 small onion, finely diced

3 tablespoons pine nuts

1 pound (455 g) ground beef (Irene prefers kosher beef)

½ teaspoon salt

½ teaspoon freshly ground black pepper

½ teaspoon allspice

FOR THE DOUGH

2 cups (280 g) fine bulgur wheat

1 cup (125 g) all-purpose flour

1 tablespoon corn or other neutral oil

1 teaspoon salt

1 teaspoon freshly ground black pepper

1 teaspoon ground cumin

3 cups (720 ml) canola oil

1. Make the filling. Heat the oil in a large skillet over medium heat, then add the onions and cook until translucent, about 5 minutes.

2. Add the pine nuts and cook until the nuts begin to color, 2 to 3 minutes.

3. Add the ground beef. Using a spatula or wooden spoon, break apart the meat as it browns. Add the salt, pepper, and allspice and cook until the meat is completely browned, about 10 minutes. Set aside to cool.

4. Make the dough. Heat 2 cups (480 ml) water on the stove until hot. Combine the bulgur and water in a bowl and let the bulgur soften, about 20 minutes.

5. Strain the bulgur in a fine-mesh sieve, pressing to remove as much water as possible.

6. Combine the bulgur with the flour, oil, salt, pepper, cumin, and 2 tablespoons of room-temperature water in a bowl, food processor, or bowl of a standing mixer until thoroughly mixed. Add additional water, a little at a time, until the dough forms a ball.

7. Pull a knob of the bulgur dough from the bowl and form it into an egg shape. Using your forefinger, make a hole in the center of the ball and fill with a heaping teaspoon of the filling, taking care not to break through the other side.

8. Close up the hole by pinching each side, and form the croquette into the shape of a football. Wet your hands if the dough begins to stick to them. You can freeze the kibbeh at this point or fry immediately.

9. Heat the canola oil in a large pot to 350°F (175°C). Working in batches, fry 3 or 4 kibbeh at a time until golden brown, about 5 minutes. Drain on paper towels.

10. Repeat for the remaining kibbeh. Serve hot.

Irene's Sambousek
(CHEESE HAND PIE)

SERVES 4 TO 6 (MAKES 9) | **PREP** 10 MINUTES | **TOTAL** 1½ HOURS

SAMBOUSEK IS A common Lebanese hand pie filled with meat or cheese. Many come fried, but Irene bakes hers, and they are delicious. I love how easy they are to make, and how you can freeze them and pop them in the oven whenever you have some last-minute guests. Any mild cheese will do for these. In Lebanon, they are filled with aged kashkaval, a hard, yellow cheese, but Irene usually uses a mix of mozzarella and cheddar (and sometimes even American).

1 cup (110 g) shredded mozzarella cheese

1 cup (115 g) shredded cheddar cheese

½ cup (110 g) small curd cottage cheese

1 large egg

3¼ cups (405 g) all-purpose flour

1 teaspoon baking powder

1 teaspoon salt

½ cup (1 stick/115 g) unsalted butter or margarine, at room temperature

1 cup (240 ml) whole milk

1 large egg beaten with 1 tablespoon water

2 tablespoons sesame seeds

1. Preheat the oven to 350°F (175°C). Grease a baking sheet and set aside.

2. Combine the cheeses and egg in a medium bowl and set aside. The mixture should be firm, not mushy.

3. Place 3 cups (375 g) of the flour with the baking powder and salt in the bowl of a food processor and pulse to combine. Add the butter and process until fully incorporated. Slowly add the milk, stopping when a soft ball of dough forms. If it's too sticky, add more flour, 1 tablespoon at a time, until it reaches the desired consistency.

4. Pull a palm-sized bit of dough from the bowl and place on a lightly floured surface. Press into a thin, 6- to 7-inch (15- to 17-cm) circle with your fingers. Place ⅓ to ½ cup (28 to 47 g) of the cheese mixture in the center and fold over to enclose the filling and create a half moon. Crimp the edges by pressing them with your fingers or with a fork. Repeat until you have used all of the dough and filling.

5. Place the half moons on the prepared baking sheet and brush the tops with the egg wash. Sprinkle with the sesame seeds. You can either freeze them at this point or bake immediately.

6. Bake for 35 to 40 minutes, until the tops turn golden brown and the cheese begins to ooze out a bit.

A still life painted by Irene of a compote dish (fruit stand) that belonged to her paternal grandparents. This dish was carried from Syria to Egypt to Lebanon. After her grandmother passed away, it was given to Irene's parents who brought it with them to Buffalo, NY.

IRENE FARHI SANKARI

Irene's Knafeh
WITH ORANGE BLOSSOM SYRUP
(Sweet cheese and Phyllo Casserole)

serves 6 TO 8 | *PREP* 20 MINUTES | *TOTAL* 1 HOUR

THIS DELICIOUS DESSERT is made of shredded phyllo soaked in butter with a creamy cheese center and a drizzling of orange blossom simple syrup on top. It's a treat enjoyed all over the Middle East. Traditionally, the cheese used is nabulsi, a soft white cheese, but Irene substitutes shredded mozzarella because it's much easier to find.

FOR THE PASTRY

1 pound (455 g) kataifi (shredded phyllo dough)

1 pound (4 sticks/455 g) unsalted butter or 2 cups (455 g) margarine, melted

1 pound (455 g) shredded mozzarella

1 cup (240 ml) heavy cream, whipped to stiff peaks

FOR THE ORANGE BLOSSOM SYRUP

1 cup (200 g) sugar

⅓ cup (80 ml) water

1 tablespoon orange blossom water

1. **Make the pastry.** Preheat the oven to 350°F (175°C).

2. Place the kataifi in a large bowl and pour the melted butter over. Toss, pulling the threads apart, until all of the kataifi is coated and moist.

3. Grease a 9 × 13-inch (23 × 33-cm) glass dish and add half of the kataifi, spreading it out to cover the bottom.

4. Distribute the mozzarella over the kataifi to create an even layer of cheese.

5. Spread the whipped cream over the mozzarella.

6. Cover the cheese and whipped cream with the remaining kataifi. The dish can be covered and frozen at this point for up to 30 days, or baked immediately.

7. Bake for 35 to 40 minutes, until the cheese is melted and gooey.

8. **Make the orange blossom syrup.** Heat the sugar and water in a small saucepan over low heat, stirring constantly, until the sugar is fully dissolved and the liquid thickens, 8 to 10 minutes. Add the orange blossom water.

9. Place the knafeh under the broiler until the top crisps and turns golden brown, 1 to 2 minutes.

10. Drizzle the orange blossom syrup over the top and serve immediately.

IRENE FARHI SANKARI

239

FETHIE ABOWEZNAH LOUTFI

◆

The old adage "Don't judge someone until you walk a mile in his or her shoes" seems spot-on when you listen to the stories told by any immigrant woman.

THIS IS ESPECIALLY TRUE OF Fethie Loutfi, a dynamic, eighty-five-year-old immigrant. Fethie's life has given her many joyous memories, but she has not been spared times of heartache, tragedy, and hardship. Most importantly, she was willing, literally, to walk many, many miles to obtain the best life could offer.

At the age of fifteen, Fethie's life changed drastically in a matter of moments. She remembers clearly when her family's goat farm was dispossessed and life as they knew it changed forever. Knowing they could no longer remain in Palestine, they left with just the clothes on their backs, walking across the desert, barefoot, with the hope of survival and a new start in a new place on their minds. Fethie remembers having to be exceptionally strong walking alongside her family; her mother carried her four-year-old brother, Ali, in her arms, while she and her ten-year-old sister, Shahdia, struggled to keep up with their father's determined pace.

After many days of travel, they arrived in Jordan and requested refuge but unfortunately, the Aboweznahs were turned away, so the family had to continue their journey. Without hesitation or rest, their feet carried them for another month, to Syria, which opened its borders to this family of refugees, who began a new life in a camp, full of hope for a new start and a brighter future.

As the oldest, Fethie had to help her mother with the family chores. She was smart and willing to work, so she immediately found full-time employment as a maid. She and her father went out daily to work. This allowed her mother to stay back at their tent and tend to her sister and brother. Her father slowly began to purchase cows with the money he and Fethie brought home and sold the milk to support the family. As Fethie explained, Syria provided them with a home and with rations of food. "Finally," she told me, "we were able to once again stand on our own feet." For this reason, Fethie still feels a strong tie to Syrian hospitality and maintains a home there to this day. Her family still resides there as well.

While in the camp, she fell in love with Abdulaziz Loutfi, an Albanian refugee, and they decided to marry in 1951. A year later, her first son, Adam, was born. Then, in 1953, they decided to leave the camp with assistance from the Catholic church and a relative of her husband's who was already settled in the United States. They first went through Lebanon, then to Egypt, then to Italy, and finally arrived in the United States on a large vessel funded by the Catholic church. The trip took one month, but this time she knew from the outset where she was headed and that the future looked bright.

Once in New York City, Fethie's husband worked to support his growing family while Fethie took care of the children. Once the children began school, Fethie found a job at the United Nations, working the "graveyard shift" as a member of the maintenance staff. She worked all night so that she could get her children off to school, pre-make dinner, and get a few hours of sleep before heading back to the UN.

To further improve her life, she also studied for and obtained her driver's license. Once she began to drive, she organized a carpool for her fellow local UN maintenance women. She drove many of the women to and from work.

While cooking maqluba (page 242), a Palestinian rice dish, with Fethie, her love for her family, the United States, and Americans was very clear. She raised eight children and takes pride in how many of them married outside of her faith. Her sons- and daughters-in-law are Muslim, Catholic, and Jewish, and she has relished spending her life celebrating all the varied holidays of her children and grandchildren.

Although this area is now a suburb of present-day Tel Aviv, it was still considered Palestine when Fethie resided there in 1931.

Fethie's Maqluba

(LAYERED RICE, CHICKEN, AND VEGETABLE CASSEROLE)

serves 6 | **PREP** 1 HOUR 30 MINUTES | *TOTAL* 3 HOURS

THIS IS A great dish for company because it yields a large amount and it's a complete casserole, with protein, starch, and veggies! *Maqluba* means "upside down" in Arabic, and this dish is so named because it is cooked upside down and then turned out for presenting. It's quite a showstopper if you can successfully get it out of the pot in one piece; "It's all in the flip," says Fethie. For another traditional variation, substitute lamb for the chicken.

2 large eggplants, peeled and sliced ¼ inch (6 mm) thick

3 cups (570 g) jasmine rice

Kosher salt

6 bone-in chicken thighs

1 cup (240 ml) white vinegar

4 chicken bouillon cubes

1 teaspoon Arabic Seven Spice (see Note, page 245)

1½ cups (360 ml) canola or other neutral oil

2 large potatoes, peeled and sliced ¼ inch (6 mm) thick

1 head cauliflower, cut into florets

1 cup (approximately 8 to 10) baby carrots

1 tablespoon plus 1 teaspoon clarified butter or ghee

¼ cup (35 g) pine nuts

1 large tomato, sliced ¼ inch (6 mm) thick

1 tablespoon finely chopped parsley

FOR THE CUCUMBER-YOGURT SAUCE

1 cup (240 ml) plain whole-milk yogurt

1 cucumber, peeled and grated

1 teaspoon kosher salt

1 teaspoon dried mint

1 teaspoon finely minced garlic

1. *Make the maqluba.* Sprinkle the eggplant slices with salt. Set aside for 1 hour.

2. Place the rice and 1 teaspoon salt in a large bowl with warm water to cover. Let soak for 1 hour.

3. Place the chicken thighs in a large bowl and cover with the vinegar and 2 tablespoons salt. Let soak for 1 hour.

4. Rinse the chicken thighs thoroughly and place them in a large stockpot. Add enough water to cover and bring to a boil.

5. Add the chicken bouillon cubes and Arabic Seven Spice, reduce to a simmer, and cook until the chicken is almost cooked through, 20 minutes.

6. While the chicken simmers, heat the oil in a medium pot over medium heat.

7. Fry the potato slices, then the cauliflower, and then the carrots in the oil until golden brown, 2 to 3 minutes each. Transfer to paper towels to drain. Keep the oil hot.

8. Squeeze the eggplant slices of excess water and fry them in the oil until golden brown. Transfer to paper towels to drain.

9. Remove the chicken from the cooking liquid and remove and discard the skin. Set aside, reserving the cooking liquid.

Continues

FETHIE ABOWEZNAH LOUTFI

of Entries is Prohibited
ata
see amendment page 6
Eyes
Brown
wife
Fuat and Faisul
Signature of Bearer
Cancelled
New Application 8-8-74
Not Valid Unless Signed By
Whom It Has Been Issued
of State of the United States of America,
may concern
to pass,
all lawful
abovenamed
States.
and and the
ent of State.

10. Drain the rice and wash until the water runs clear.

11. Heat 1 tablespoon of the clarified butter in a large, nonstick pot over medium heat until melted, then add the drained rice and stir to coat. Cook, stirring, until the rice begins to swell, about 5 minutes. Transfer the rice to a large bowl.

12. Heat the remaining teaspoon of butter in a small sauté pan over low heat, then add the pine nuts and cook until golden, 2 to 3 minutes. Set aside.

13. Place the vegetables in the large nonstick pot, starting with tomato, then eggplant, potatoes, cauliflower, and carrots, making a decorative pattern. Sprinkle half of the toasted pine nuts on top.

14. Layer half of the buttered rice on top of the vegetables, spreading to cover.

15. Place the chicken in an even layer on top of the rice.

16. Cover the chicken with the remaining rice, and then pour enough of the reserved cooking liquid into the pot until the rice is just submerged. Take a plate that's just slightly smaller than your pot opening and place it upside down on top of the rice.

17. Cook, covered with the plate, over medium heat until all the liquid is absorbed and the rice is cooked, at least 1 hour.

18. Remove the pot from the heat. Carefully remove the plate covering the rice.

19. Let the pot cool for 15 minutes. Place a large, sturdy serving platter larger than the pot upside down on top of the pot. Flip the pot upside down onto the serving platter. If possible, have a friend assist in holding the heavy pot and plate as you rotate and place them on the counter. Tap the bottom of the pot to release.

20. Sprinkle with the remaining pine nuts and parsley.

21. **Make the cucumber-yogurt sauce.** Combine all the ingredients for the cucumber-yogurt sauce in a small bowl, and serve alongside the maqluba.

Note

If you cannot find Arabic Seven Spice, blend 1 teaspoon each of ground black pepper, ground cinnamon, ground cumin, ground coriander, ground cardamom, ground cloves, and 2 pinches of saffron. Use 1 teaspoon of the blend for the recipe and reserve the remainder for another use.

RECIPE INDEX

◆

INDEX

♦

ACKNOWLEDGMENTS

When I fully realized the amount of work it would take to
complete this book, I joked that it must take a village
(of immigrants) to get a cookbook done. As with all great projects, one
person may take the lead, but there is always a team of people
working close behind who help make it happen. I am so incredibly
grateful to *my* village: the people who believed in me,
understood my vision, and helped me every step of the way.

◆

First and foremost, thank you to **THE TALENTED IMMIGRANT WOMEN** who contributed to this book. Each one of you opened your home and your heart to me, not only by sharing your secret family recipes, but by inspiring me with your stories, perspective, and grit. I am in awe of your courage, strength, and love for your families. Thank you also to your children and grandchildren who coaxed each of you into the kitchen with me. There is an immediate bond between first gen kids, and I feel it now more than ever.

To **PHIL**, my partner in life. You give me the courage and the space to follow my dreams, and your quiet strength has led me to accomplish things I never thought possible. You are my best friend and I love you.

To **ALESSANDRA**, **VERONICA**, and **DANTE**, who inspire me to be the best mother I can be. You are my three biggest accomplishments in life and I love you with all my heart. I live to make you proud.

To **MY PARENTS**, who have made me the woman I am today. Dad, you have always believed in me and supported me, regardless of the task. Your love and knowledge guide me through every challenge I face.

Mom, I can only hope to be half the mother you are. Thank you for teaching me to cook and for making the best meatballs in the whole wide world.

To **LUCIANA**—God only gave me one sibling, so he figured he would give me the best one ever created. You are my rock, my constant cheerleader, and the person who will always tell me when I'm wrong and why I'm right. Thank you for being you.

To **CHRIS**, whose generous heart opened the first door needed to get this book to the finish line. I often think back to when I told you I wanted my blog to be turned into a book, and when you said, in true Brooklyn fashion, "I know a guy."

To "that guy," **BRAD THOMAS PARSONS**, who took my call and offered advice, guidance, and knowledge that empowered me to believe that I could really do this. You are a rare breed, Brad—you root for the success of others, and I will be forever in your debt.

To **SARAH SMITH**, the best agent a gal could ever ask for. You took my call and answered every email, even when this big tree was only a little seedling. This project never could have happened without your belief in it. Thank you for giving me the map and for being my incredible copilot for this project!

◆

254

To **ANDREW SCRIVANI**, my fellow paisano. Your passion is contagious, and I knew after our (more-than-one-hour) introductory call that we were a match made in heaven. The beauty of each photograph and the way you made every woman feel so special prove that you are an artist of the highest caliber, and you and that special woman running around your studio have a place in my heart.

To my editor, **CRISTINA GARCES**, thank you for just "getting it." You read beyond my words to help this book say what it needed to, and most important, believed it needed to be said. You answered emails at lightning-fast speed and took my calls when I was panicked and needed to be talked off the ledge. After our first meeting, you said that we would make a beautiful book together, and damn it, we DID! I will always cherish making pernil with you and Haydee.

To the rest of the **HARPER DESIGN TEAM**, especially **LYNNE YEAMANS** and **ERIN SLONAKER**, you made this book, and my words, better and brighter than I could ever have dreamed possible. **FALON KIRBY** and **CHRISTINE CHOE**, thank you for getting the book out the door and into the hands of as many people as possible.

To **JILL BROWNING**, who jumped in with both feet and got this book the attention it deserved.

To designer **LAURA PALESE**, who took the components of what would make a beautiful book and multiplied that by a thousand. I will never forget the first time I saw the sample pages and literally lost my breath. Thank you for creating an heirloom-quality book I am so very proud of.

To **ALEXANDRA UTTER**—from the first day of culinary school when you said, "Are you from Westerly, RI?," to buying me spoons for the final, to cooking with me for my in-laws' wedding, to giving me Andrew's digits, you are truly a BFF. Wherever I go, I hope you will always be cooking on the burner beside me.

To **MONITA BUCHWALD**, whose precision and ability to figure out the matrix of any recipe was priceless when dealing with the many head-scratching methods we deciphered for this book. As an intern in the MSLO kitchen, I was immediately inspired by your grace and knowledge, and your generosity and talent helped to make the recipes in this book foolproof.

To **KOSTAS CHELIOTIS**, my brother from a Greek mother—you responded to that first fateful email within seconds, signing up your mother, Nelly, to be the first woman to cook with me. Once I had Nelly, I knew I could really do this.

To **JENNIFER ITSKOWITZ**, for all my Insta fame.

To **AMANDA HESSER** and **MERRILL STAUB**, thank you for giving me the courage to put my ideas on paper and the advice for how to get it done. Food52 has taught me so much, and I am forever grateful to be a part of your big, extended family.

To **HANA CHOI**, my first and best partner in culinary school. You have the uncanny ability to make a stranger feel right at home and looked after. Words cannot express how grateful I am to all the opportunities you make sure I land. Love to love you.

To **KERRY DIAMOND**, for believing this project was "so Cherry Bombe" and for all your love and support.

To **GABY CASCANTE**, my GPS to the universe. Your advice and guidance get me through each and every day.

To the **NEW CANAAN COOKING** and **BAKING FACEBOOK PAGE**, especially to the people who stepped forward and gave my recipes a whirl. You (and this book) prove that home cooks are the best cooks.

To **AMANDA CANN** and the whole **INTERNATIONAL CULINARY CENTER COMMUNITY**, where it all began. ICC is really where dreams become reality, and to have a built-in cheering section is quite nice. I cherish you and all that you do.

◆

ABOUT THE
AUTHOR

◆

ANNA FRANCESE GASS grew up in a small town on the Rhode Island shore
before moving to New York City for college and an exciting new life. After a stint
in the corporate world, she decided she needed to spend her time in the kitchen,
not an office cubicle, in order to be truly happy. She quit her fast-paced sales job
and enrolled in Culinary Arts at the French Culinary Institute (now ICC) in Lower
Manhattan to follow her dream of professional cooking. Soon thereafter, she
found her niche in test kitchens; she has worked for Whole Foods, Mad Hungry,
and Martha Stewart Living Omnimedia. Currently she is a regular contributing
editor and recipe tester for Food52 and contributing writer for msn.com. She has
also assisted on numerous successful cookbooks as a recipe tester and has worked
behind the scenes on several cooking television shows. She also actively works
with food companies to promote, test, and develop recipes for their products.
She lives in Connecticut with her husband and three children. Follow her on
Instagram @annafgass and on her website, www.annasheirloomkitchen.com.

DATE DUE

JUN 24			
OCT 17			
			PRINTED IN U.S.A.